3D Pen: Colour & Construct

#1 Fairy Houses
& Fantasy Gardens

By Angie Scarr
& Frank Fisher

Dedication

This book is dedicated to Rosie. Rosie - you can get pleasure from creativity even if it isn't high art ;-)!

Publishing Data

First published 2018 Sliding Scale Books (SSPB07)

Plaza De Andalucia 1, Campofrio, 21668, Huelva, Spain.

Contents

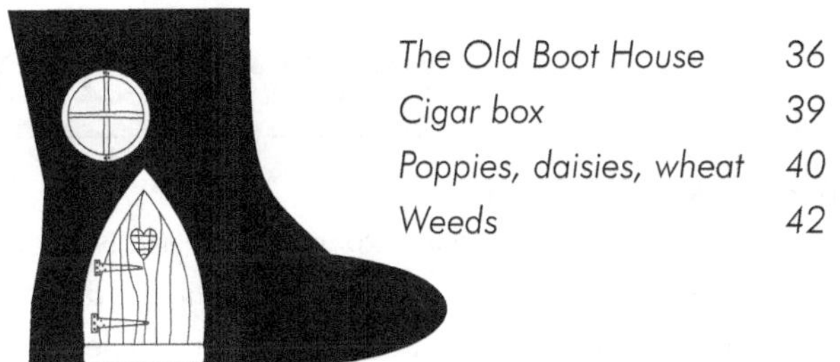

Introduction

The great thing about fairy houses as a miniature subject is that you can mix your scales in any way you like. You can suspend your disbelief and set your tiny house among full size plants and flowers or make the plants and flowers tiny too. You can also steal full size elements to add to your construction just as a "borrower" or a fairy might do! The grass can be longer, the windows bigger than scale. Proportions really don't matter in the fairy world. This is an exploration of the fantasy world of fairy houses that can set a miniaturist free from convention and as such I've had a lot of fun doing it. I hope readers of my polymer clay books will enjoy this new fantastical adventure with me and enjoy adding a new tool to their creative equipment. It's important that your fairy houses aren't too perfect. After all, a fairy wouldn't build their house with pre formed slabs of concrete but more likely with twigs and leaves and pebbles and whatever he/she would find lying about the woodland floor including rubbish!

How to get started

What you will need

A 3D pen. You don't need an expensive pen at this stage. It's a bit like learning to write or draw. It's not important to spend a lot of money on a pen at this stage. Try to get one with a variable temperature but you don't need to go into the high end ranges for this. See the suppliers list at the back of this book for suggestions. The pen I use in this book is the Idrawing 3D pen model ID-361 which at the time of writing is inexpensive and functional.

Filament

An assortment of coloured filaments suitable for your pen. Please note that some pens only do a small temperature range. This means you have to choose filament that is suitable for your pen's temperature range. Most (at the time of writing) use ABS 1.75mm, but the pen I'm using in this book has a dual temperature control so it can also use PLA. However new safer, more environmentally friendly products are being invented all the time for the 3D print industry and the pens will, I'm sure, follow this trend.

To start with get a bundle or two of short lengths in assorted colours.

For this book you may wish to source some of the more natural greens although for fantasy scenes some people like the brighter colours. Some companies offer a reasonably priced pack of sample lengths in various colours. There are also companies that specialise in single sample lengths. And some who sell filament as very short sticks. You will also need some wood filaments. These do melt at a lower temperature so you really do need to wear a mask (see below) if your pen doesn't have a variable temperature!

The biggest problem you will have if you want 'real' greens for example, is sourcing all your materials from one supplier.

The companies who sell short lengths have a better range of colours but this is the most expensive material per Kg. On the other hand a beginner may find the short lengths useful for small pieces.

As you start to do more work you will start to get 'annoyed' at some of the filaments which can sometimes 'pop' and 'part' in the middle of drawing. I would only recommend really good quality filaments like Rigid Ink for example, but unfortunately you have to cross into other makes to get a reasonable colour range. Supplier info is in the back of this book. If you have real difficulties contact me through my webpage.

A face mask with a carbon filter. Currently as far as I can see none of the pen manufacturers recommend this but though this is currently not the recommendation on any of the pen packs, I believe in the future it will be. I very strongly advise the use of a mask. And plenty of ventilation especially if using the pen in a communal area. You can also buy small extractors which seems like a good idea.

A working board and/or a transparent glass surface to work on and some surface adhesive treatment. Recommendations in the supplier list.

Access to a photocopier or a scanner and printer.

Other tools

Small snippy scissors for removing hairy bits of filament from finished work. A palette knife for removing work from your work surface.

Other materials

Cardboard packaging tubes or empty custard powder/cocoa powder tins. And lots and lots of clean empty Tetrapak cartons (UHT milk and juices come in these).

Indelible pens and pencils for copying designs onto Tetrapak surfaces etc. or altering designs

Scissors for cutting out and assembling 3d designs.

Masking tape for taping down designs, assembly and masking off areas etc.

You may wish to use mesh armatures to keep your houses strong. Mesh can be bought at pet shops as it is used for animal cages. This can be cut with strong scissors or tin snips.

Drawing surfaces and methods.

Choose your working surface

For flat drawings I have a piece of MDF 54 x 42cm to tape my double page spreads to. That gives me plenty of space and I can even add other little bits of extra elements to the side such as extra fruits or flowers to work on concurrently, for example if I don't want to keep changing the colours but I do want extra parts for the hop bines and the brambles for example. I work on my lap as its the most comfortable position for my arms. If I'm using a glass surface I have a glass door from Ikea's cheap-bin shop. You can sometimes get clear glass chopping boards or table covers in toughened glass which will work just as well.

Flat drawings

Firstly, you're going to need to photocopy the page anyway. Because you don't want to ruin your book and you may want to do the same item over and over again.

Then you can choose which method to go for depending on the design and the effect you're trying to achieve.

1) Working directly on paper. Tape your paper down to the surface you're working on and draw directly over the paper. The positive is that there's good adhesion to most papers. The negative is that there's too good adhesion to most papers making it difficult to peel off afterwards. You can soak the paper off however and a toothbrush will help you remove the last traces of paper. The downside is that this can be time consuming. Another plus for using paper is you can use the outlines of the prints to enhance your design as the ink is picked up by the molten filament. This works particularly well when making the dragonfly on page 45.

2) taping tracing paper over photocopy. Tracing paper of certain kinds can resist adhesion a bit more than paper and that can be useful for removing work later but also makes it a little more difficult to get your work to stay in place.

3) Using glass surfaces

You can now get spray and paint on coatings that help stick the filament to the surface. Otherwise the filament would just slide off as you try to draw. I've used Sennelier's Fixatif but many more products are becoming available. 3DLac, Dimafix, and MagiGoo. Apparently you can use the following Hair Sprays: L'Oréal Studio Pro "Boost It", L'Oréal Elnett Satin, or glue sticks including: Wizard, Q-Connect, U-Stick, UHU, Pritt Stick. I haven't tried any of these. Masking tape your paper under the surface and then you can work directly on the glass. The surface coating may need to be reapplied after each piece of work though and this can be tiresome waiting for the coating to dry..

4) Specialist mats

Mats (usually silicone) are now being developed with patterns ready indented into them. They're OK but silicone surfaces can be a bit tricky to adhere your work to especially when new. They are also currently rather expensive

5) There is however another option with a lovely hold and removal result. Tracing your design on to the silver inside of a Tetrapak carton. Milk and juices come in Tetrapak cartons. The surfaces both inside (silver) and outside (printed) make excellent adhesive surfaces but release easily without leaving residue , or without leaving much residue in the case of the printed side. The inside has a particularly good surface for drawing on and you can press through a photocopy with a pencil to leave visible marks to work on. It can also be used to make the inner and outer 90 degree corners and v shaped formers for certain designs, for example butterflies (page 44) and 3D stems for bushes. For simple designs this is by far and away the best option so start washing out your Tetrapaks now! You can cut the tops and bottoms off. Cut down the seam to open them out. Remember to throw the bottle top end into the plastics recycling where they accept Tetrapak cartons.

Colouring In

Filling in the patterns with 3D pen filament is a lot like childhood colouring in. It can be frustrating and pleasurable in equal measure. You want to fill each space as cleanly as you can while still recognising the limitations of 3D pen. You will never get a completely clean smooth look without resorting to infilling with other materials or sanding down etc. and to my mind if you want that look you should be going for other materials anyway! So lets work with the nice 'scribbly' material that we have and work with its abilities rather than against them.

Its helpful to think of the techniques for colouring in small and medium sized shapes as a little like embroidery. There are several ways to delineate the sections. You can either outline them in a different colour and then push the next layer right up against or even over the lines. Or you can use different directions of pen strokes to give extra texture or you can overlay an outline of a different colour to give a cartoonish look. One more thing you can do to accentuate separate elements in the same colour is to draw over with a hot pen nib without extruding any more filament.

Making 2 types of line

If you want a line of filament allow the tip to extrude the material as you pull the pen away from it. If you want a flatter line you need to push the tip through the material as it extrudes. (e.g. grass on page 21)

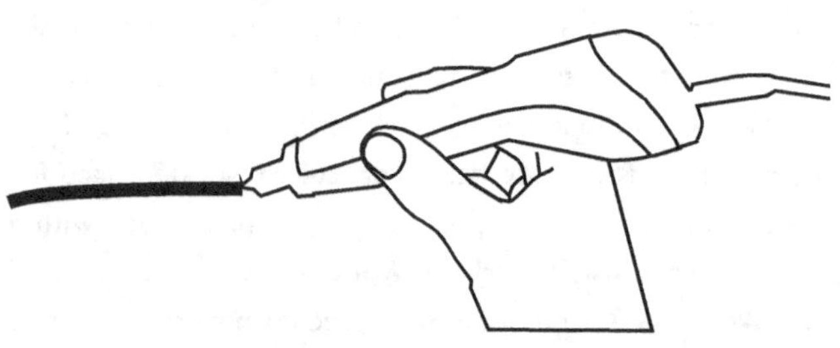

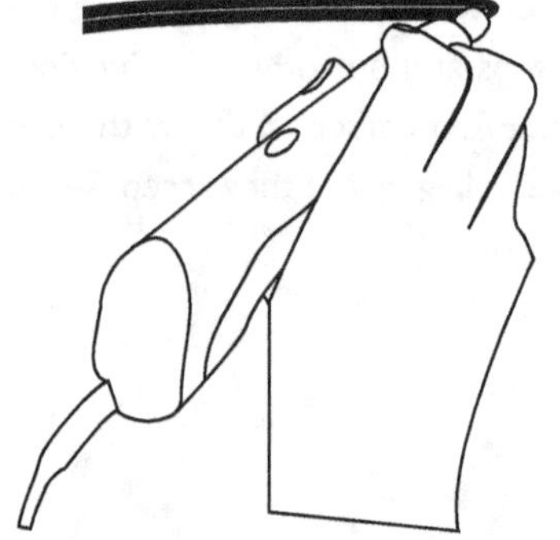

Infill methods

When building up small or larger areas of colour on to a surface here are some of the movements you can use

Straight lines stopped at one end. Feeding the filament only for the one down or sideways motion of the pen. The feed is then released and then the next line is laid up against the first so that the hot plastic fuses. When done more separately and more firmly it separates the filament into two. Or at least makes it very thin in the centre. I discovered this when making grass and if the feed is released at the end of the stroke it can even cause the tips to curl. This can be quite attractive but it does need to be anchored (started) on a thicker area of work.

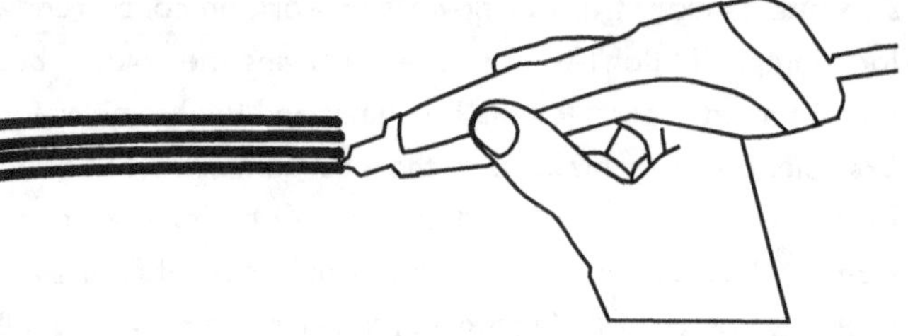

Straight lines continuous this means keeping the feed going as you return to your start point in both these cases the lines sit side by side and you will get a cord effect.

Straight lines pushing the pen tip through the hot plastic. That is to say angle the tip so that the feed extrudes in front

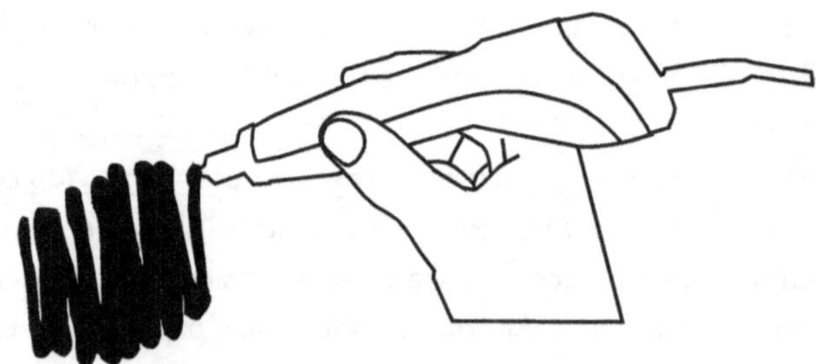

of the tip and continue pushing the pen forwards. When done lightly this flattens the filament. I use this one for infilling leaves and flowers. It leaves a fatter border which can mean that you can make fairly delicate flowers like poppies. The edge is thicker and more stuck together, therefore reinforced.

Figure of eight. Similar to straight lines. When practised and with the feed set to fast (if you have a pen with a feed speed setting) this can be one of the quickest ways of filling large areas with a fairly thick layer of filament.

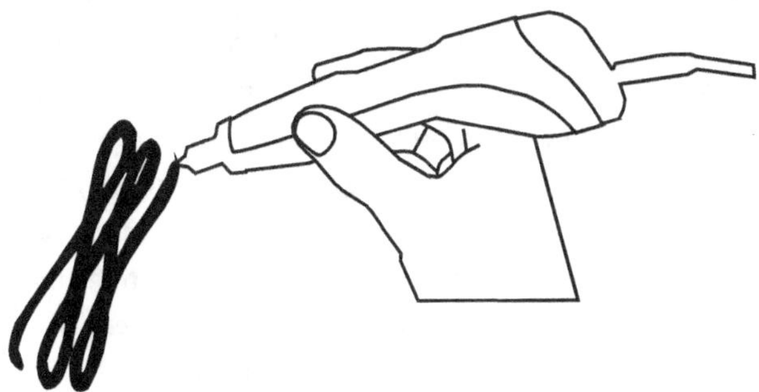

Dots can be made if your pen has the tendency to feed hot plastic even without the feed pressed. I use this technique in the poppy to add dots round the edge of the centre. If you

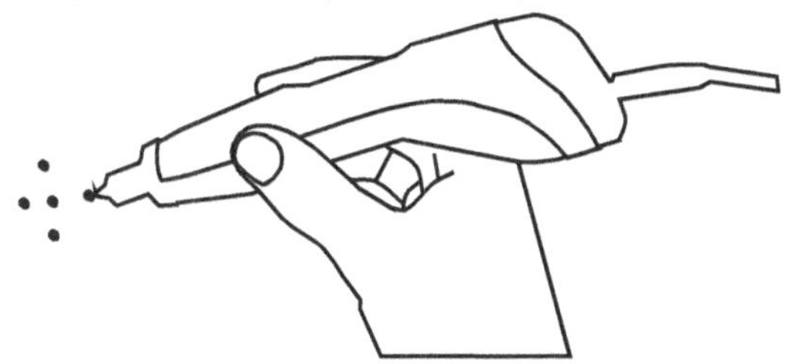

want more feed you can practise pressing the feed very quickly but this takes quite a lot of practise. Or setting the pen to a higher temperature but of course this can produce potentially toxic fumes, so I can't recommend this.

Loops are made by dotting the pen over and over in lines or randomly with the feed pressed. This is really useful to add depth and texture. I used this to good effect on the tree house. Very tiny loops just give a dotted texture. If you need to create a much thicker surface using less material you can overlay deep loops. The drawback of this is that your work can be translucent. This can also be a benefit in some cases!

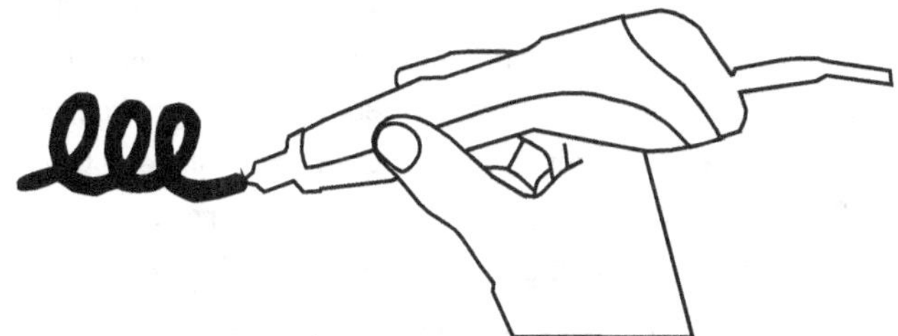

Extruded blobs. If you press your pen tip on a slight angle and allow the filament to extrude it extrudes inside itself and pushes itself into a blob. I use this in small flowers and for berries like the redcurrants and brambles.

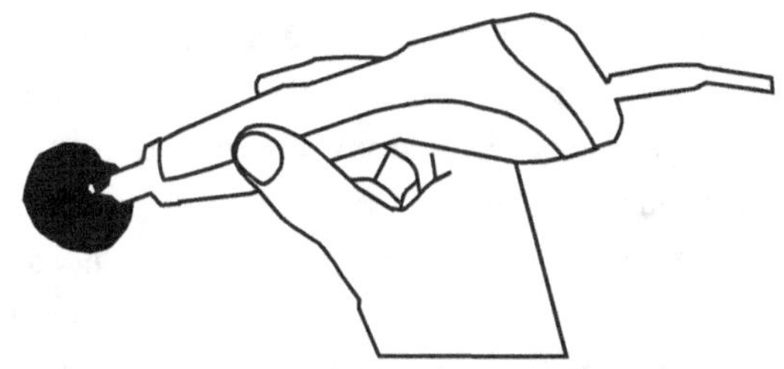

Other fills used in this book

Zig zag fill
(for stems)

Fan shape fill

Squiggle fill

Spiral fill

Armatures and supports

For round houses the supports I use are cardboard food packaging such as custard powder 'tins' and you can use cardboard packaging tubes. You can also use tubular water or pop bottles (stuffed with paper) or glass bottles. For the tree house branches I used cardboard tube from the centre of a cling film roll. The important thing is to use the correct diameter. These numbers are printed on the original designs. Obviously if you size them up, or down, you will need to use a different diameter of support. You can of course pad slightly small tubes out by adding extra layers of cardboard.

Originally I formed the rectangular house on milk/fruit juice Tetrapaks. I love these for using with 3d pen because the filament sticks to the slightly waxy feeling plasticised coating but comes away reasonably cleanly whereas paper surfaces tend to stick to the plastics and cause them to be difficult to remove. You can of course wash these off using a toothbrush to remove stubborn bits of paper..

You can work directly on to an armature with the design taped or traced on to it, or work freehand on to an armature. Animal cage wire is very good for this and can be cut using strong scissors and bent into shape (wearing gloves of course). As mentioned above for boxy shapes Tetrapak cartons make good shapes for houses. When using mesh you need to get your first layer on to the mesh. This can be the trickiest thing and I find a wrapping motion works best but a layer of paper taped on can be even better.

A note on recycling. Bag up all your left over bits and mistakes etc. You may use a variety of materials that have different compatibilities for recycling but you can store a bag of bits until they decide how to process them! Recycled filaments are currently in development.

Going 3D

Of course your pen is called a 3D pen so lets not stay on the surface! Lets start constructing! The houses in this book are joined together freehand and in mid air often without a support except the pieces you've recently constructed themselves. For example the sides of the square house and the cigar box can simply be done by holding them together at the correct (right) angle and overlaying a thin layer of filament. I do this like a spot welder by gently dabbing the surface and allowing the melted filament to fill the corner. Be aware that new hot filament will soften old filament and fuse together with it.. Great in this case! But not so great when working with really delicate plants when it can make pieces wilt or bend. So you may need to consider having some kind of rest to hold things in place while they cool. Sometimes bending filaments is exactly what you want, like when you bend the heads of a flower over (daffodil for example), sometimes you don't want them to bend over and have to be very careful how you support them while attaching pieces. Sometimes you have to put a blob of melted filament on a flower part, then rapidly add the next piece. In many cases I've left a hole in the middle of a flower so you can simply hold the petals together and apply the attaching filament in the middle and build up the flower centre freehand. Sometimes this isn't possible and you have to practise 'gluing' together tiny elements as fast as possible. This is when 3 hands would be more useful than one. You can get a soldering tool that holds elements in place or of course you can resort to actual glue ... but where's the fun in that?

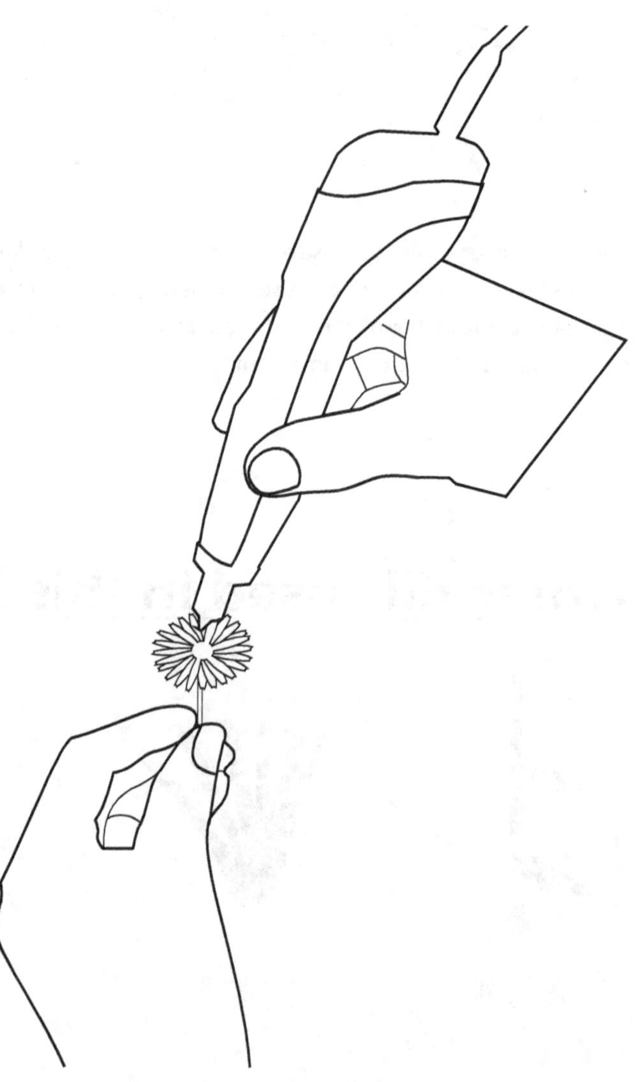

Stone house howto

On the following pages you'll see your first big project. It's quite a difficult one to start with but filling in is a useful skill to gain and if you do the roof of the house first, you'll get some experience and because its supposed to be straw and supposed to be rough its a really good place to start.

You'll need a clean Tetrapak, scissors, a thin spatula, masking tape and straw or grass or twig coloured filament. I used TreeD's 'Sandy'.

1) Photocopy the page and tape to a flattened Tetrapak carton so that you can cut out the shapes of the big ¾ circle. You need to cut this piece out as it is needed to make a curved former. Cut out the triangular holes. Also cut out the large and small rectangles and the little chimney cover on page 10 You can discard the paper afterwards as the Tetrapak material is the best to use in this case.

2) Bring the two straight sides together to form a shallow cone with the printed side on the outside of the cone. The printed side of the Tetrapak sticks more firmly than the silver side and so is the best to use for your first project. Stick with masking tape.

3) Load up your 3D pen and starting at the outer edge draw the pen towards the centre by an inch or a couple of centimetres or so. Slowly and surely at first draw backwards and forwards as if 'colouring in'. Try to put each filament touching the next one. If you have a rapid feed it will stick better. Continue round the ring. Remember that because it's circular the inner edge will overlap more than the outer edge. Don't worry if this is your first attempt and you constantly get 'stringing' if you move away from the surface or snagging when the hot pen end touches your last line. Just carry on and if necessary you can snip off any stray bits later.

4) When you have done the first ring start another which slightly overlaps the first. This way you build up the whole roof towards the middle. Don't forget to leave the holes for the chimney and the windows.

5) Insert the fat triangles using the edges to tuck under the roof and tape to it. Build up the 'dormer window' roofs. Remove the roof former using a spatula. If you notice any big gaps fill them with more filament.

6) Cut out and tape the large and small chimney pieces slot the small piece into the larger one and tape them all together to form a kinked chimney. Cover them in black filament. Be careful not to hold the tube close to where you are working or you may burn yourself. Remove the tubes using a thin spatula.

Now tape the chimney cover and bend the slot pieces so they will slot into the main chimney. Build up the filament as thinly as you can. If you find this piece difficult leave it until you have more experience. Insert it into the roof and stick from the inside with more filament.

Now its time to have a go at the main house

7) Photocopy and cut out the 2 house pieces. Tape them together (with masking tape) on to a custard powder tub or similar. If your tube is bigger or smaller than mine you will have to adjust it and add your own stones. But remember that one edge needs to be left un-joined so you can remove the tub and paper afterwards. I made the stones first by building up layers of white in concentric circles (or near circles) and then filled in the mortar in grey.

8) Choose a colour for the door and window frames and do them next. AND don't forget to make the roof window frames while you have this colour in your pen. Add them into the roof using extra filament from inside.

9) Then make the door using smooth top to bottom strokes. If your hand is not steady by now its a good idea to make it in wood filament so it looks like rough wood. The hinges and handles are delicate and difficult. You can make them separately and add later.

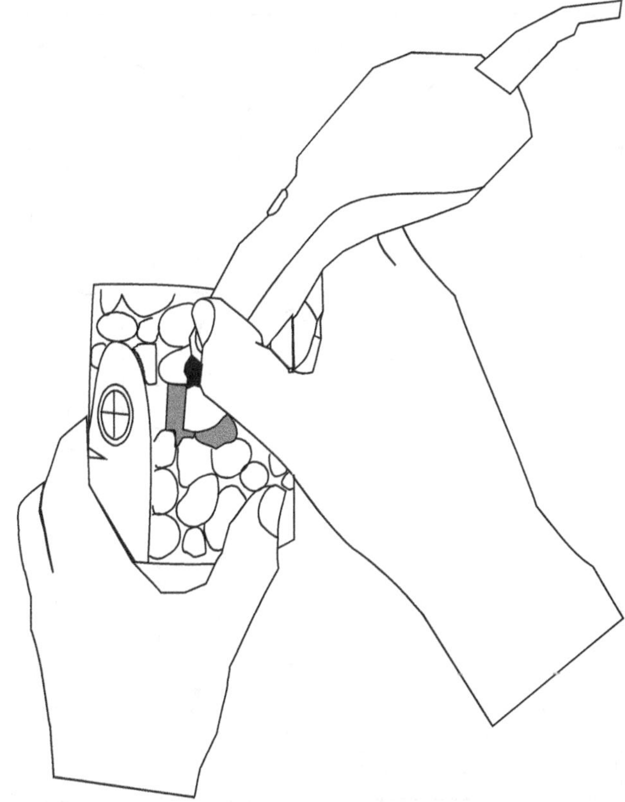

Stone House

For assembly instructions please see page 9

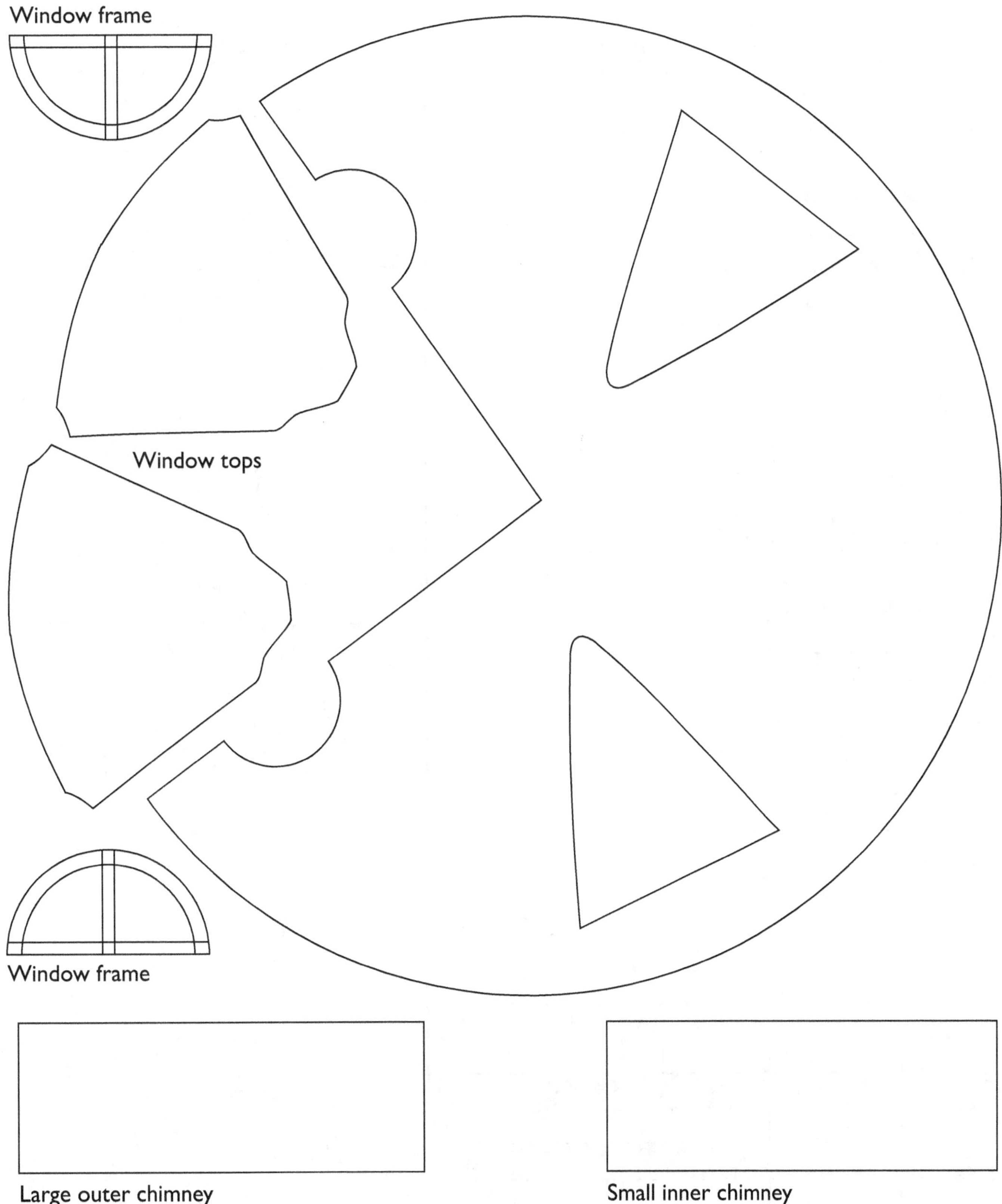

Key to picket fence

Layer 1 cover the entire drawing

Layer 2 top layer redraw on top of the grey uprights

Stone path

infill in green (grass)

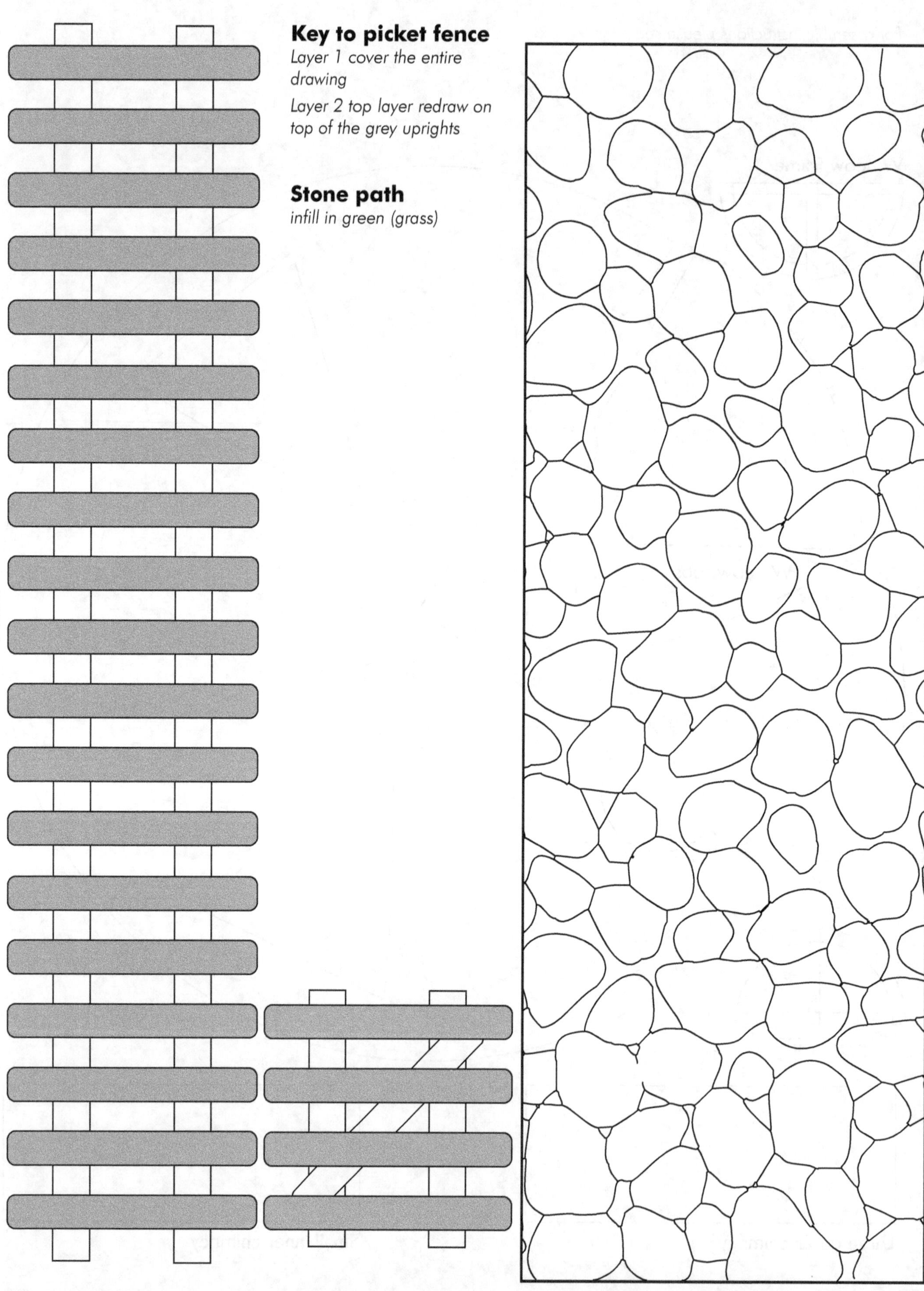

Gerbera and Daisies

Lets start making flowers

1) Draw several calyxes

2) To make the flower stems I use un-extruded (raw) filament and attach the calyx to the top using a little more green filament.

3) While I'm using green filament I fill in the petals using long straight smooth diagonal strokes from the edges to the veins. If you want to wire the plants put the wire on the central vein and cover in filament. You can also choose to make the veins another shade of green (or whatever fantasy colour you choose!)

4) Draw the 2 (or 3) layers of petals and attach them to the calyx using the central colour.

You may need to use leather gloves to protect your fingers. Children should be assisted with this process.

5) Build up the centres using the repeated short loop technique explained on page 7

6) Attach the leaves to the base of the stem. Leave a short piece of stem under the leaf to stick into the ground!

Build plants up by 'gluing' parts together using more filament. Add a central colour to the flowers after sticking together. You can draw the stems or use unextruded filament.

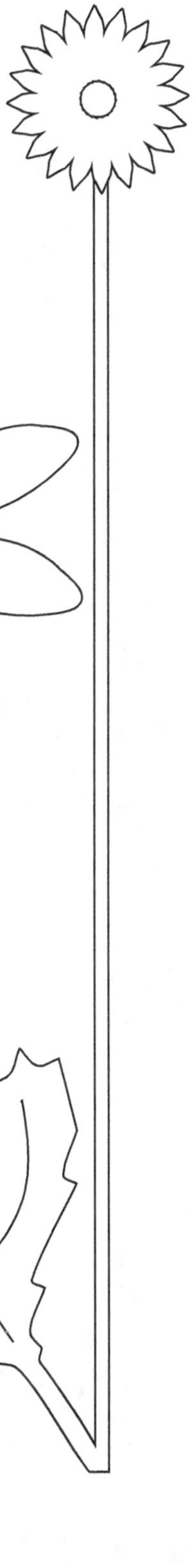

calyx

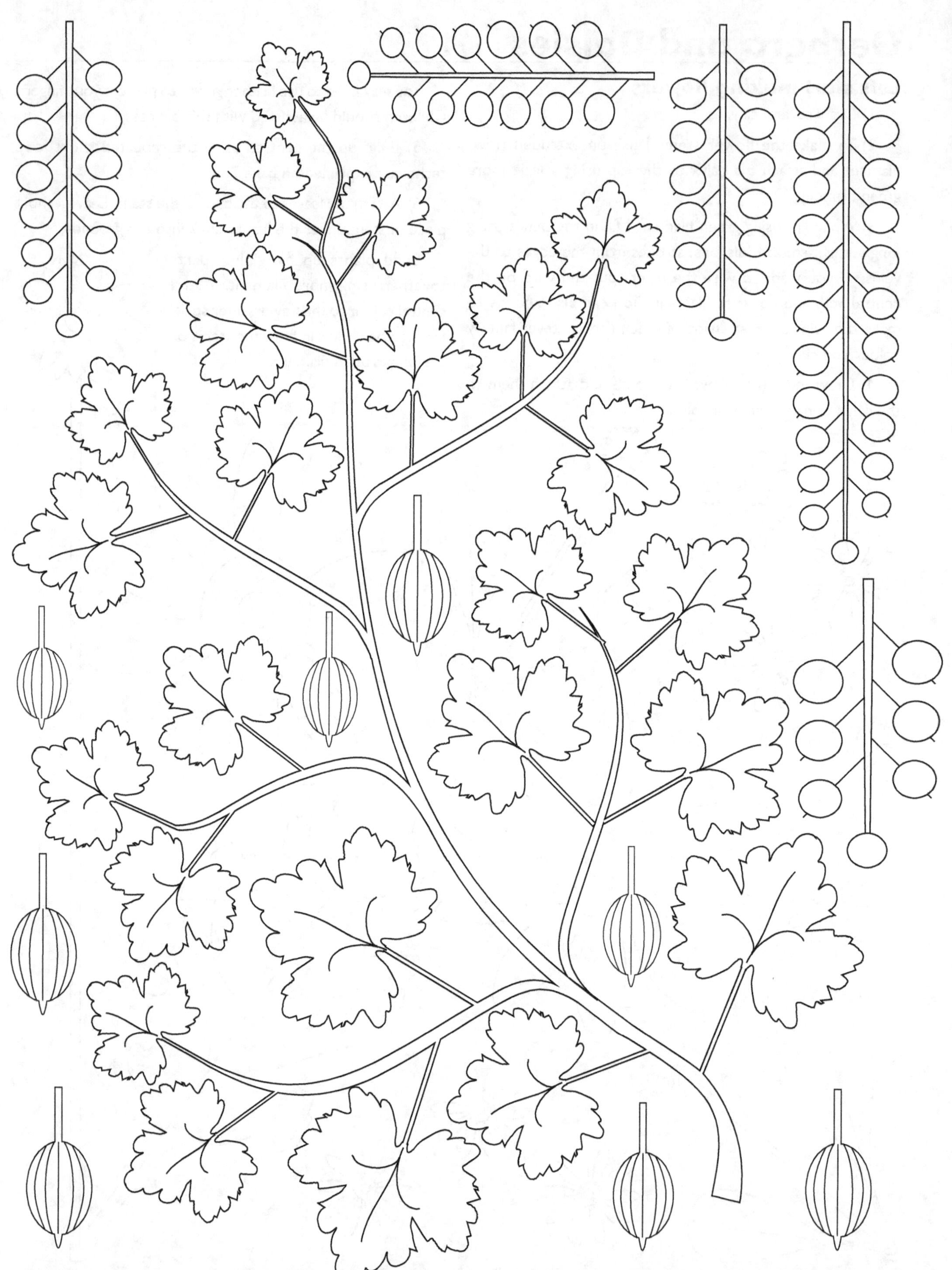

Fruit bushes

We've chosen to make one simple design for all the currant bushes and the gooseberry as they do have related shaped leaves.

For the plant draw the leaves before the stems. First draw the veins in the leaves and then infill each section using diagonal strokes.

Draw the stems before drawing the currants.

To make the fruits you need to learn to make a small 'ball' of filament. To do this set your pen to a hotter setting and press it against the surface as you extrude filament it should 'blow' a bubble of filament. This takes practise.

The gooseberries need to be made of a semi translucent material. Draw the lines after filling the space and build up until you get a nice rounded (half round) shape. Then add the lines. If possible 'glue' 2 halves together with the pen.

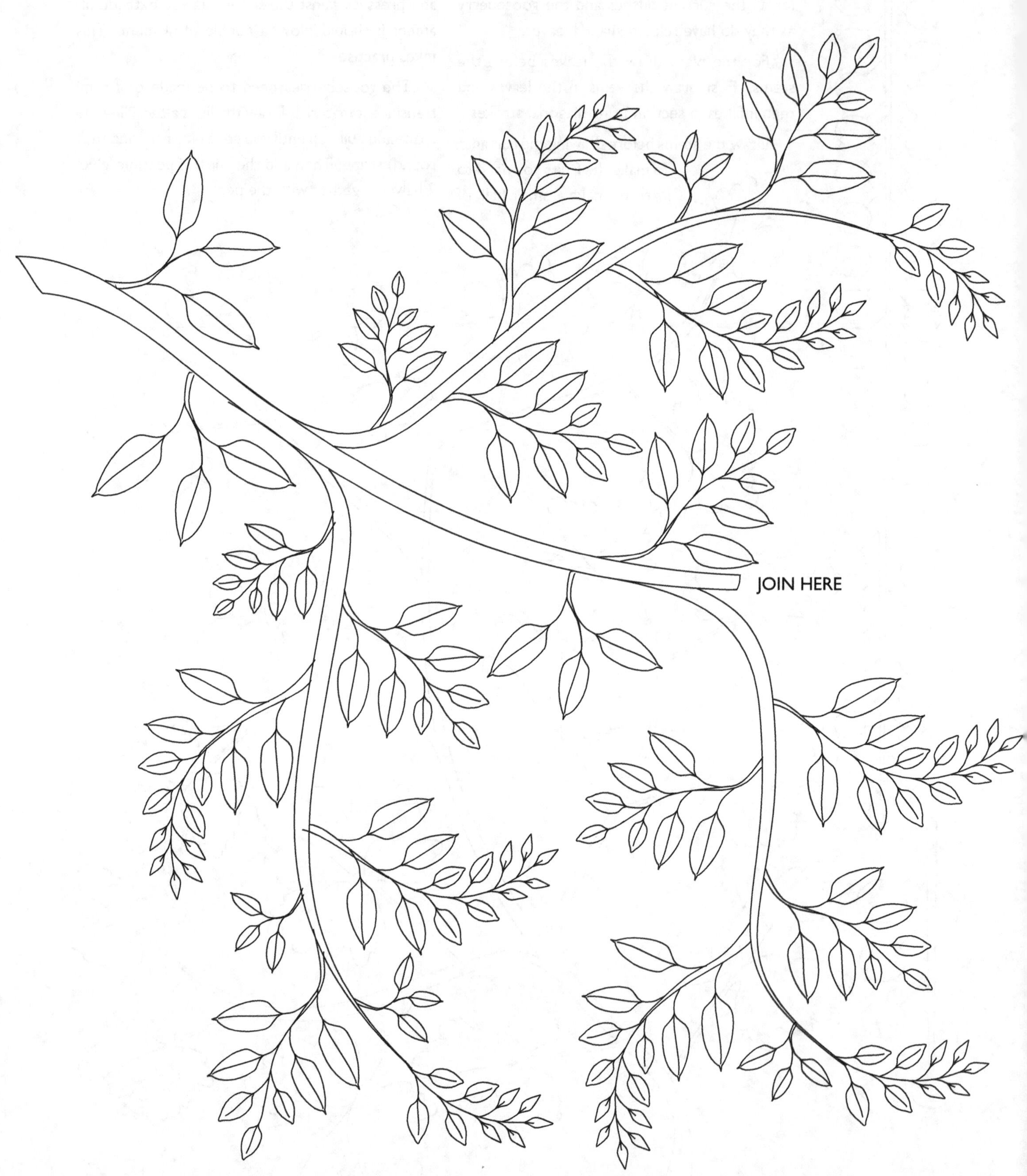

JOIN HERE

This is a double page of 'infill' plants with a simple standard leaf shape. They can be used as part of a bush or tree or the individual parts can be used anywhere in your scene. It will also give you practise in making very fine elements where you need to work quickly and confidently. You can either leave them empty or fill them in. Don't expect them to be beautiful and perfect at first. Mine certainly aren't! If you have several different greens you can play with putting them together.

Rectangular House

1) Draw the wood beam supports in wood filament and infill in whatever colour you like!

2) Stick each piece to its neighbour using the edge of a Tetrapak for support and simply drawing an extra line of wood filament in the join. Make sure you do it slowly leaving enough filament to stick it well. Choose frame and door colours and follow the lines making sure you either leave a gap between slats (which you can fill from behind, or overlapping one layer a little

3) On page 20 you will find the leaf roof. You'll need to do the 4 lines of half leaves twice for both sides of the roof. The easiest way to do them is to draw on to Tetrapak make sure each leaf sticks well to its neighbours. Lift these lines and put to one side.

4) Make the 'ridge' leaves (the whole leaves) bent over a whole empty Tetrapak. Lift from the tetrapak using a spatula to release from the surface.

5) Assemble the roof by starting with the bottom layer at the edge of a square box Tetrapak (1 litre of milk often comes in these) stick the second layer overlapping the first at the joins between the leaves (using your pen). Then the third and fourth set of both sides before adding the ridge back on. The roof should simply pop on to your house.

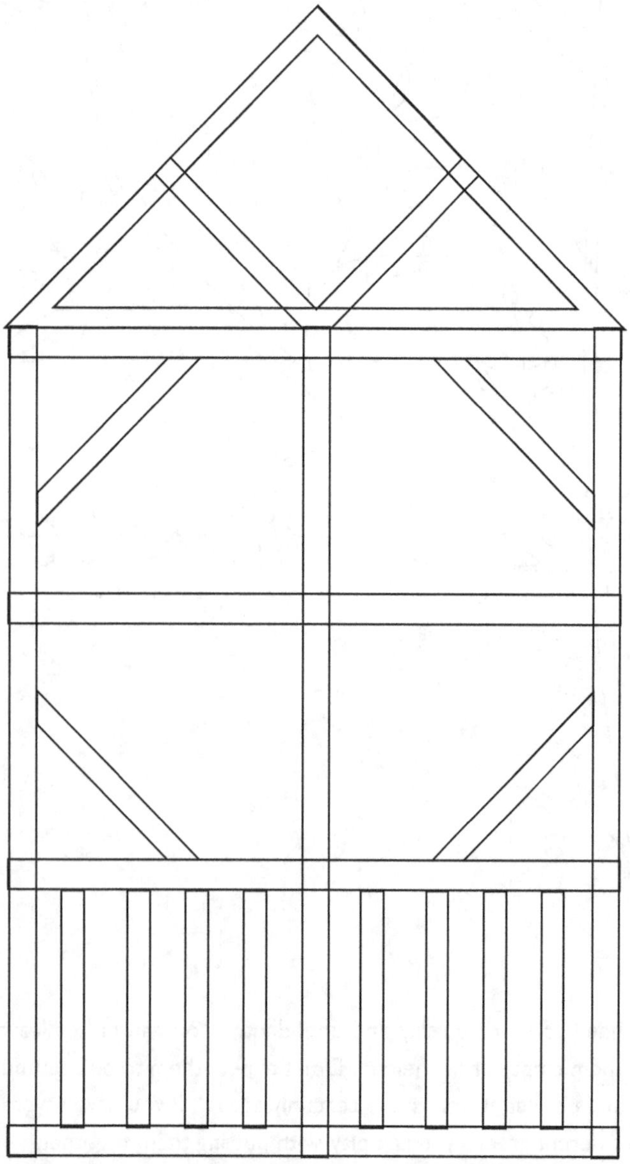

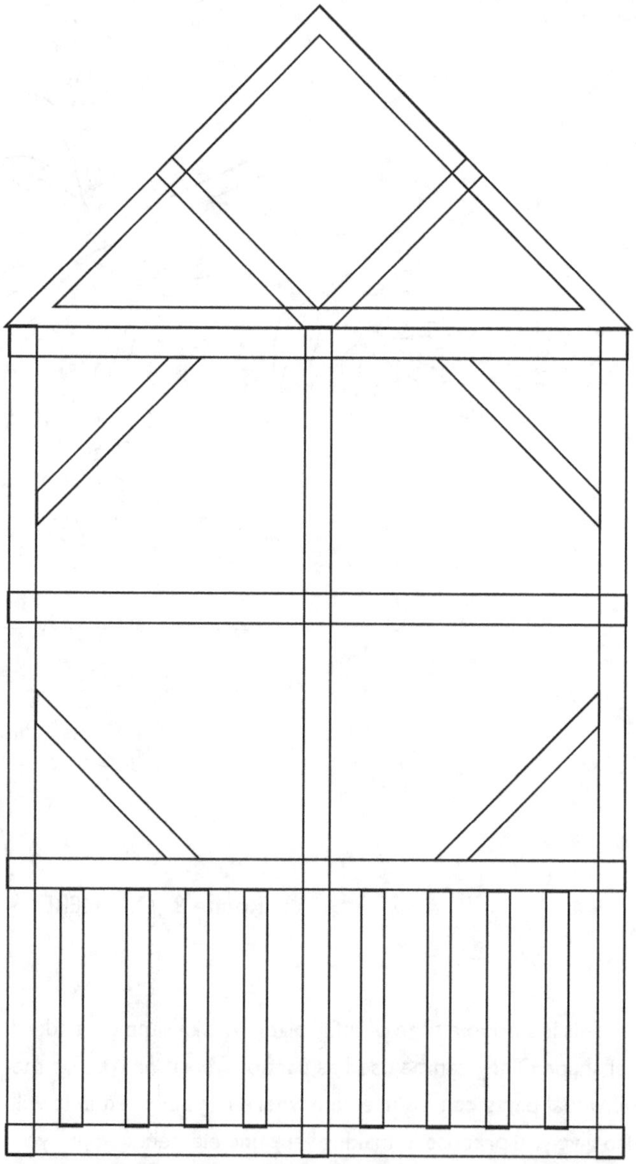

ridge leaves

roof leaves make a copy of all 4 for each side

Making grass

First build up a base layer (scribble) using short strokes of the pen on the bottom edge of a Tetrapak or paper backing or on a baseboard. Then start rapidly drawing the pen firmly up the board and then pull off at the same time as releasing the feed button, so that the pen tip flattens and divides the filament. You will find that often the ends of these grasses will even curl giving a really pleasing finish. If you want a whole meadow of grass I suggest you make several flat layers and then stick them together or make rolls from these flat grasses. You can also wrap grass around the base of your fairy house. Once you have got used to making grass you won't need a template.

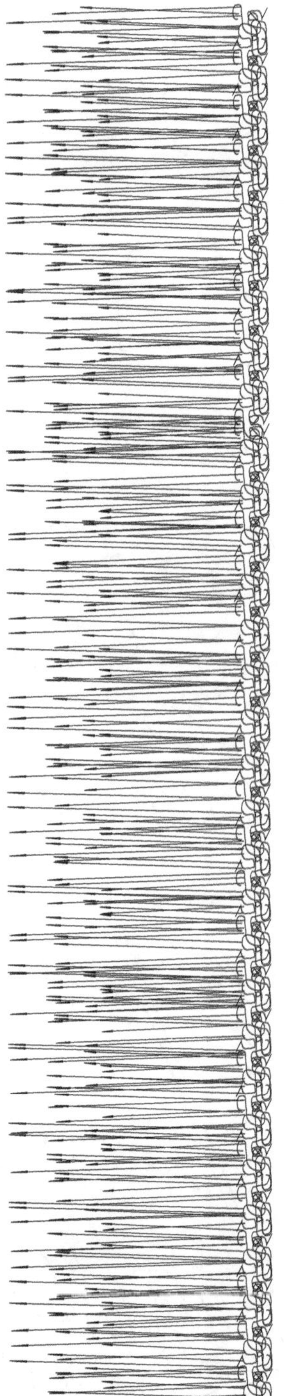
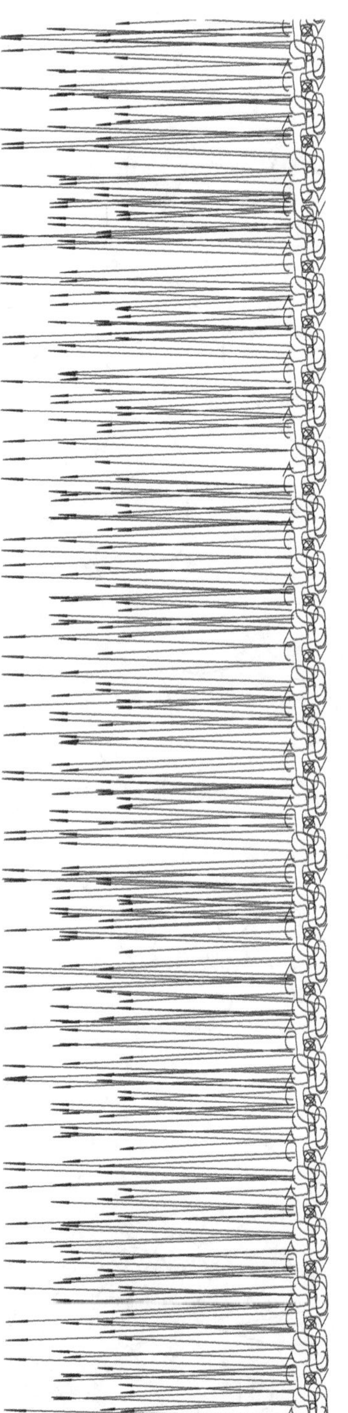
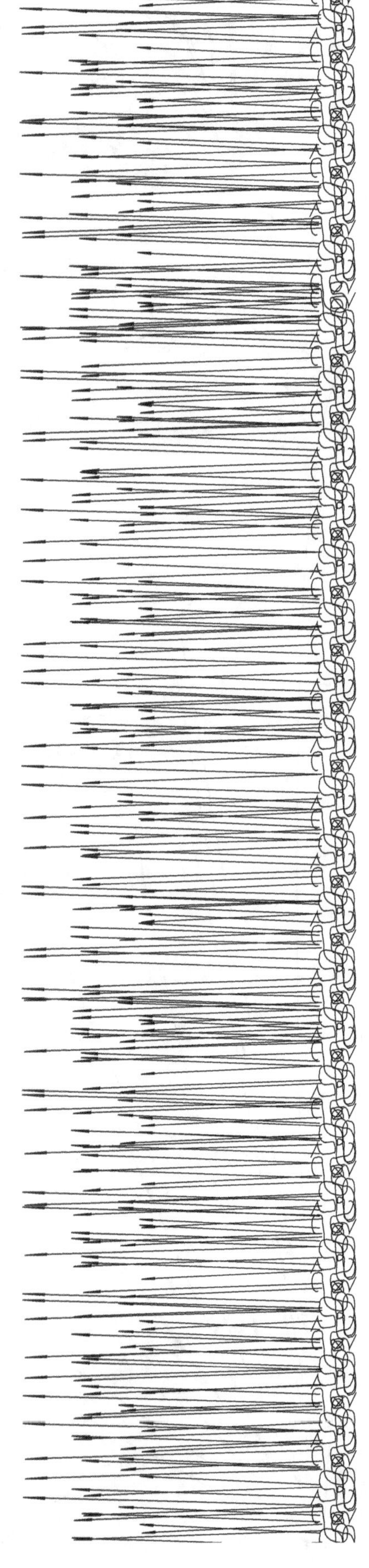

Now we're starting to get quite complicated and 3 dimensional although most of the parts are still drawn on a flat surface. The centres of the daffodil and smaller narcissus are shown as flat curved pieces on the left hand side above the daffodil plant, they need to be taped into small cylinders and covered in filament before removing them. The plant stems are only shown in place for their length and I would use solid filament. You may need to straighten the filament under heat and the daffodil would be even better made with a fatter filament. To make the daffodil calyx which is very 3 dimensional wind a 'bead' of filament round a cocktail stick. The violet flowers are made in 2 parts. First draw all the 4 petalled flowers, then the leaf that attaches to the centre. The centre is white with a little yellow at the top, and possibly ink marked. The stems are bent before attaching to the flower. You can bend gently over a hot pen tip.

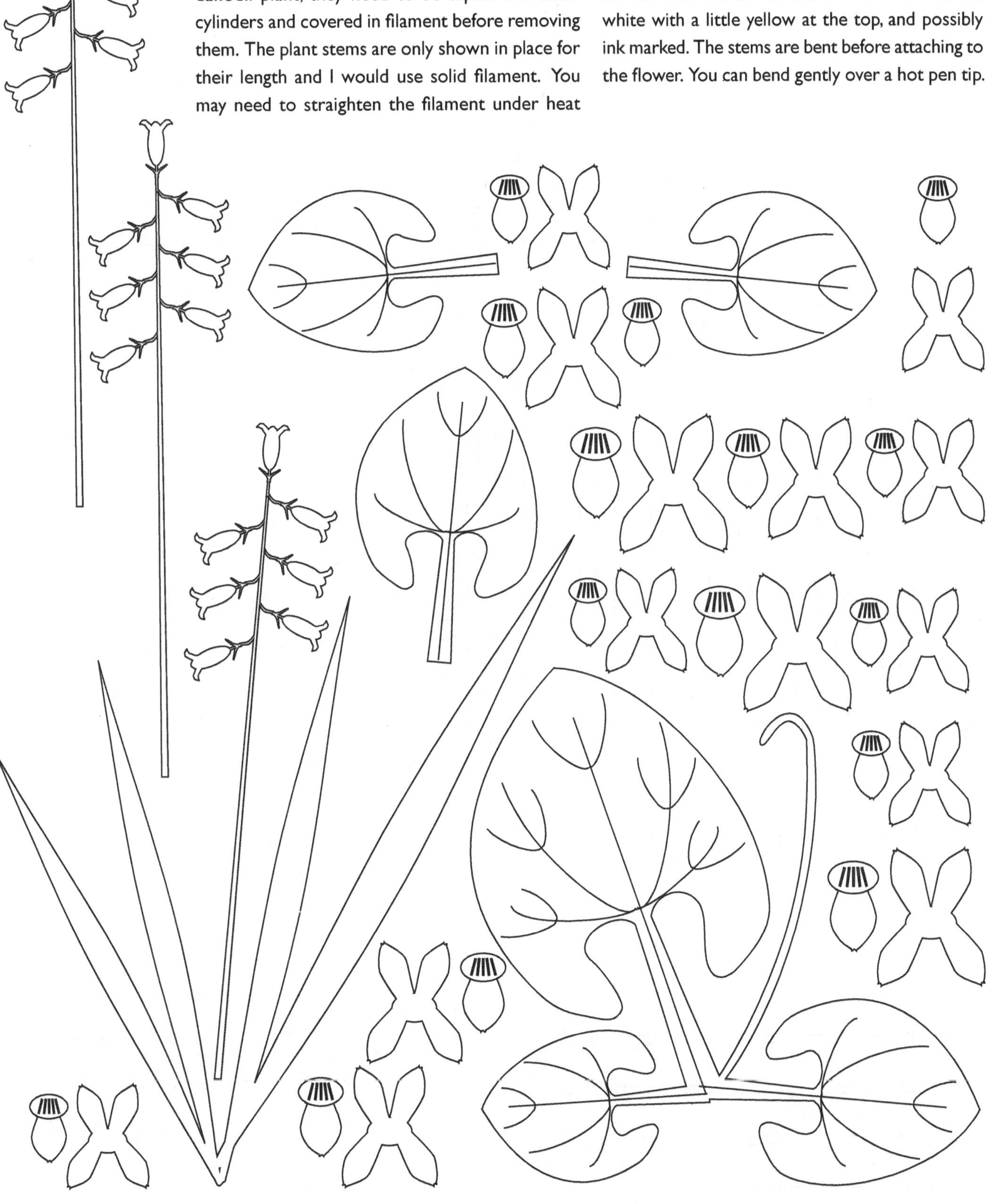

Garden Furniture

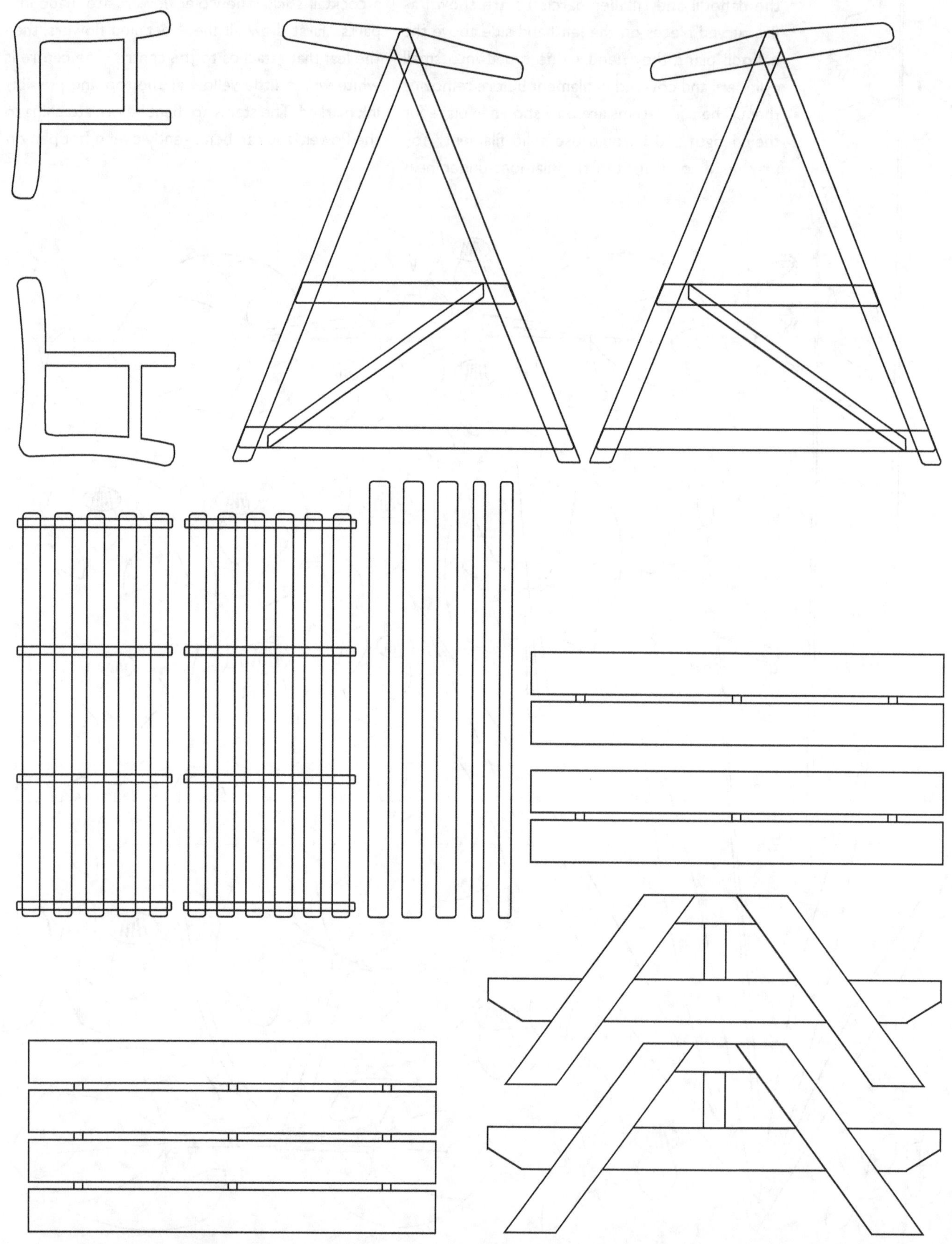

Brick path & garden furniture

I did the brick path for this house as terracotta but you could choose to make them stone colour. I used a grey filament to simulate mortar in between. This is a nice project to practise pen control and I recommend you do it BEFORE the furniture. Use a nice regular straight line continuous movement to infill the bricks and then do the mortar afterwards. This one is probably best done on paper because the paper left on the back will help to hold it together.

The furniture is best done on Tetrapak card so it peels off. I did mine on paper and the time taken peeling the paper off is probably more annoying than the time taken tracing the pattern through to the Tetrapak (silver side). I used Ice Filaments' Barnyard Brown wood filament. Make sure you do your work on this in layers and make it as deep as you can be bothered to do but I'd do the main elements 3 layers deep with the crossbars just one or two layers deep.

When you have drawn all of it, the picnic table is easier to construct. Just find something rectangular like a book. Put it flat on your work surface. Put the table top upside down right up against the bottom edge of the book and put the legs on to the underneath using the book to create the 90o degree angle. Using hot filament 'glue' the inside of the top to the inside of the leg. Leave it to cool before turning to do the second size. Then turn it the other way up to add the plank seats. This is another time when you need to work quickly. Add hot filament and press the seats on to the arms of the cross pieces.

The swing seat is quite fiddly and difficult. If you find it tricky to make straight lines a flat knife or metal ruler edge will help you make the first line in each 'slat' and then you can follow the first line. Assemble the seat onto the seat sides. Then construct the main frame using the supports. Wide supports in the centre top, bottom back and centre bottom. The thinner supports are the front and back canopy. I haven't made a canopy cover but you could. I used thread and tiny jewellery loops to hang the seat but you could simply tie it with thick sewing thread.

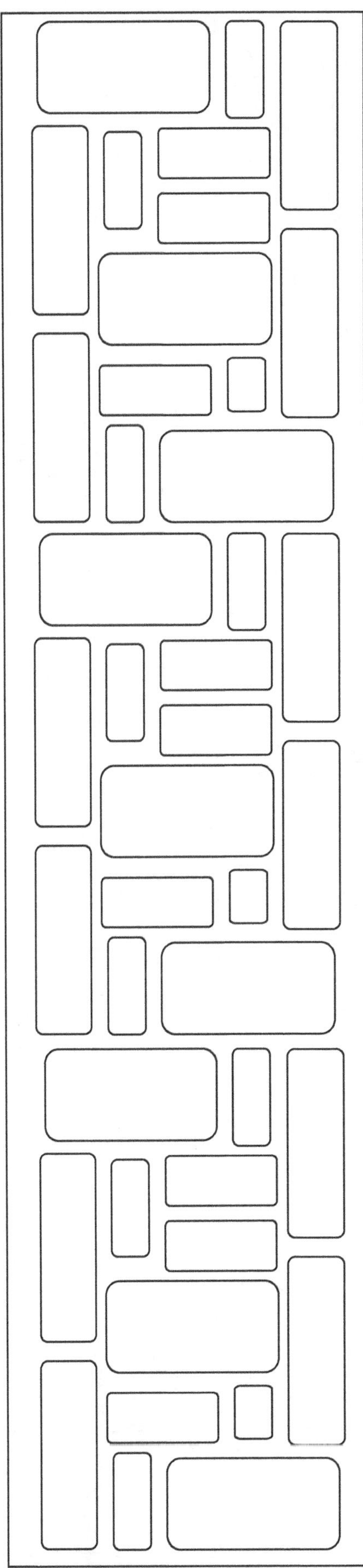

Tree House

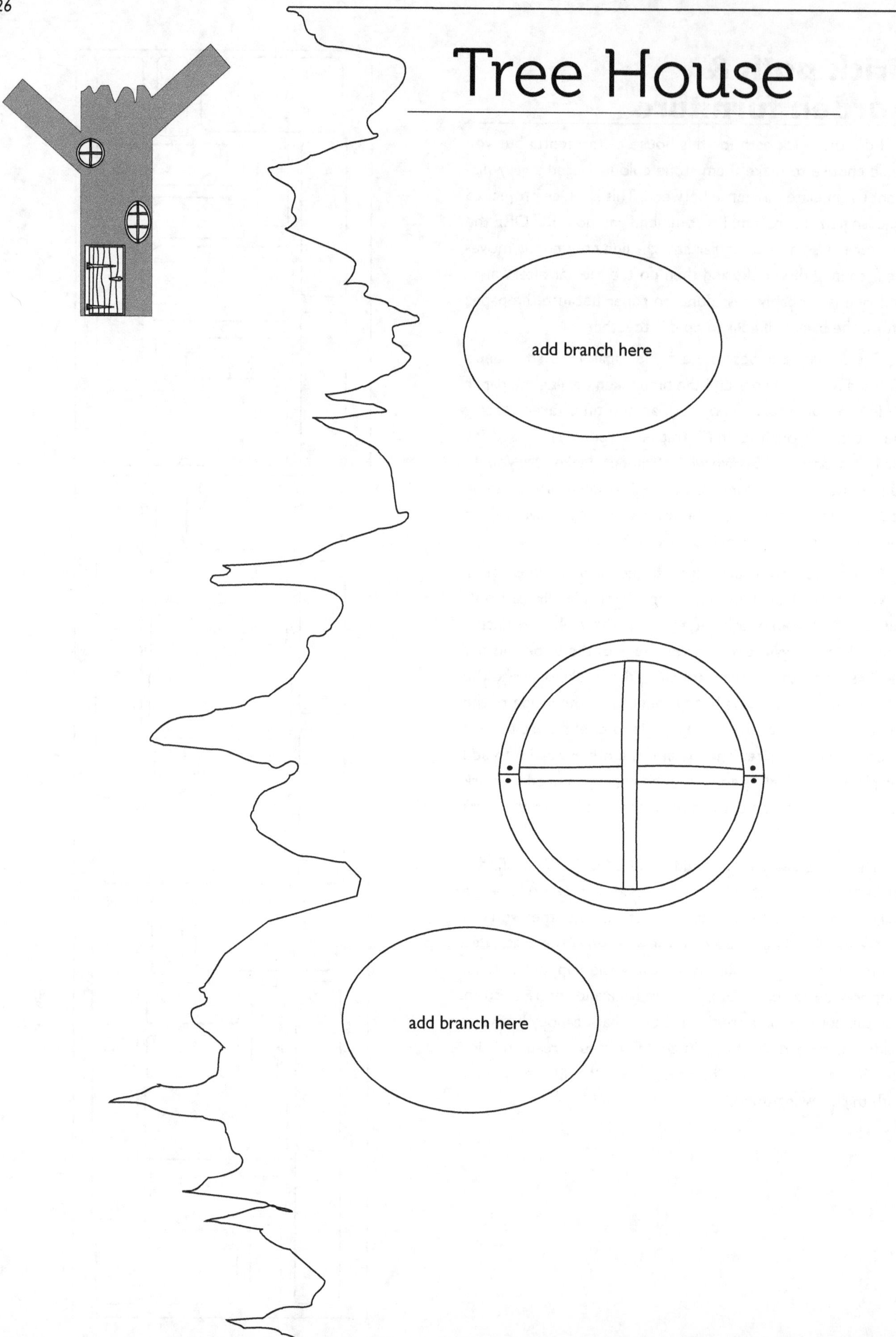

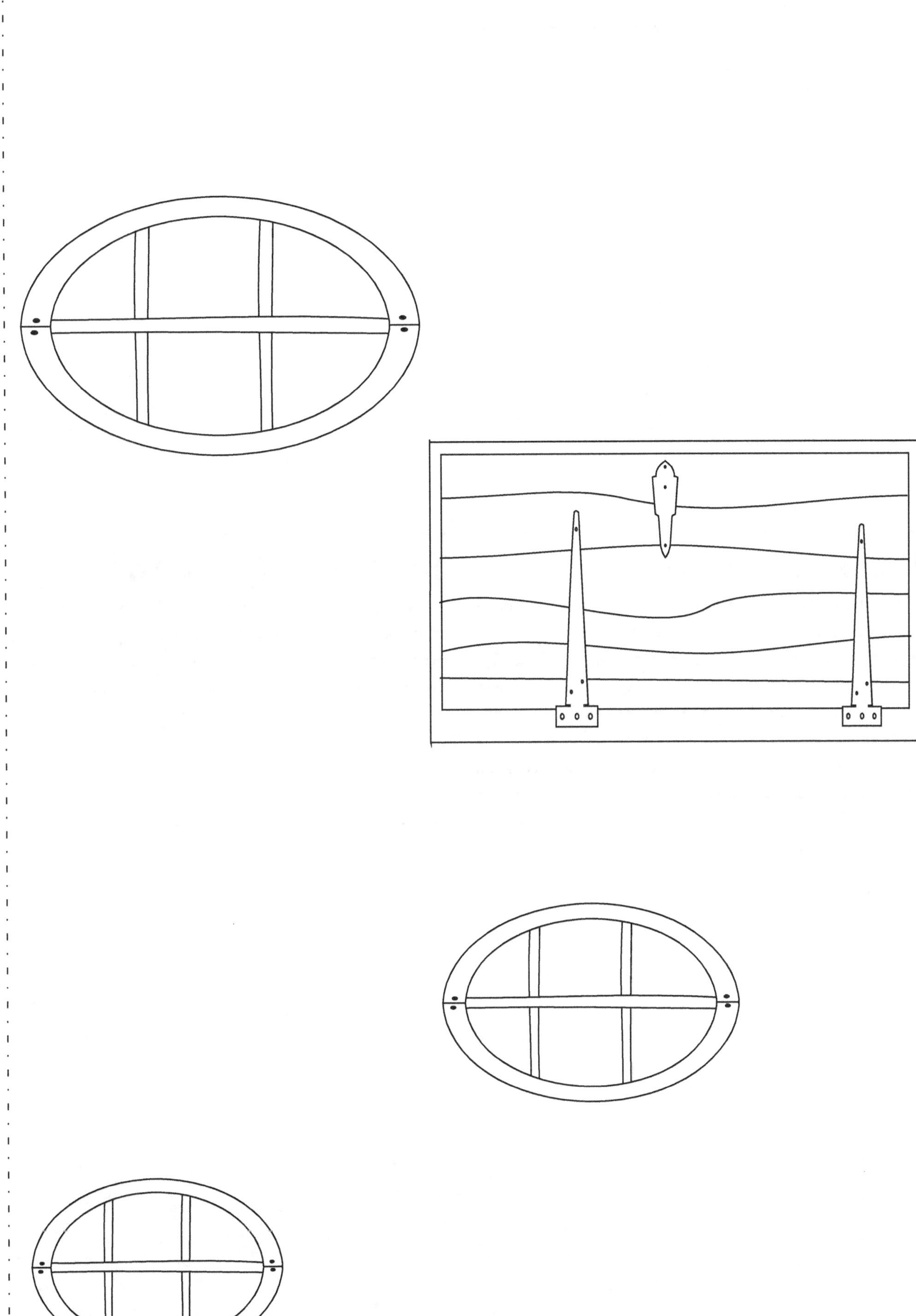

Join or adjust width here
Join or adjust height here

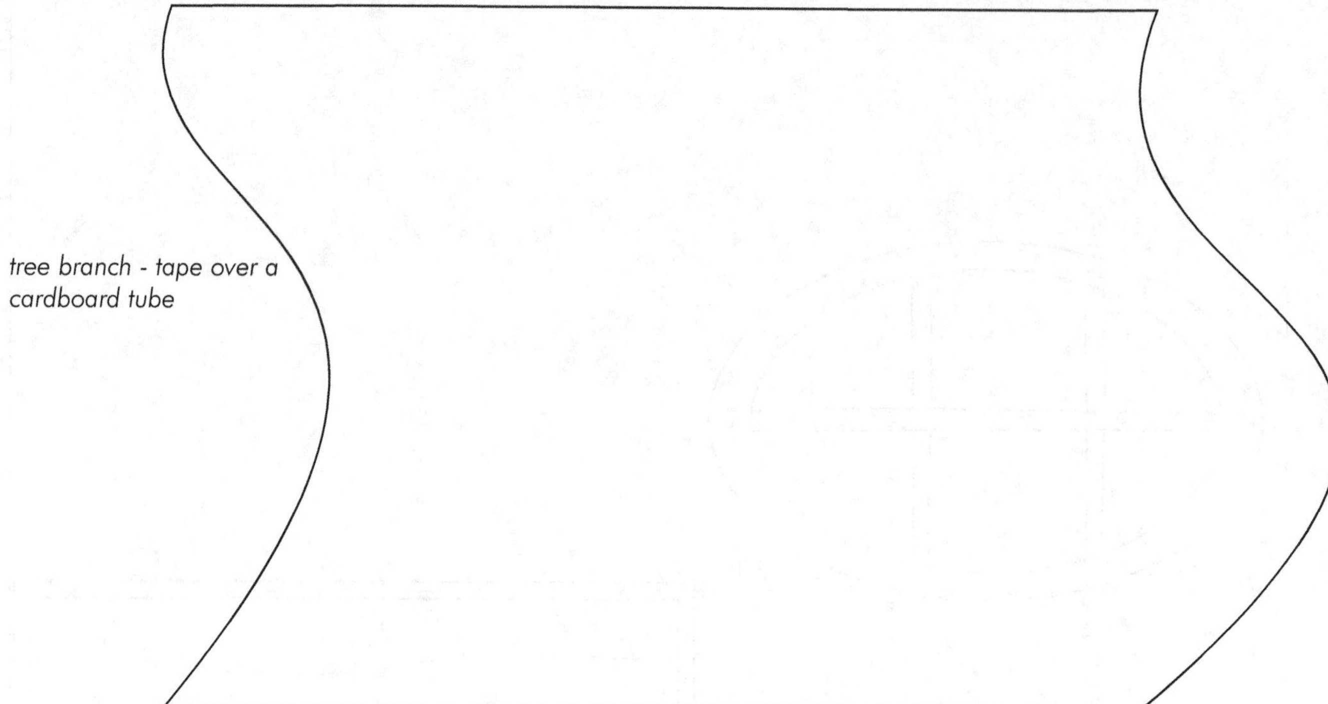

tree branch - tape over a cardboard tube

Tree branches

Build the tree house on a postage tube. Wrap the paper round the tube. You may have to alter it for size. Build on the paper and tear and soak the paper off afterwards. To build up the bark I used alternating pen work between smooth drawing with the pen pushing through the filament to flatten it and a short repetitive loop pattern to form a rough surface. The branches were built on the cardboard centre of a cling film roll. Add the branches to the upper holes once the house is complete.

To make the roof

Group the half leaves on p29 into 3 on a slight downward angle and stick together then gather the long leaves up and put over the top, showing the first layer between each leaf. You may wish to wire the leaves to make them curve more easily.

tree branch

This page introduces building 'blobs' to produce semi-3D elements you can, when you are practised, make them half round and stick 2 together. But even as semi-3D they are pleasing to make and to look at. Start with the hops. I used Rigid Ink's lovely greens: olive for the leaves and khaki for the drying hops. Fill the leaves in sections which gives a pleasing look where the sections join.

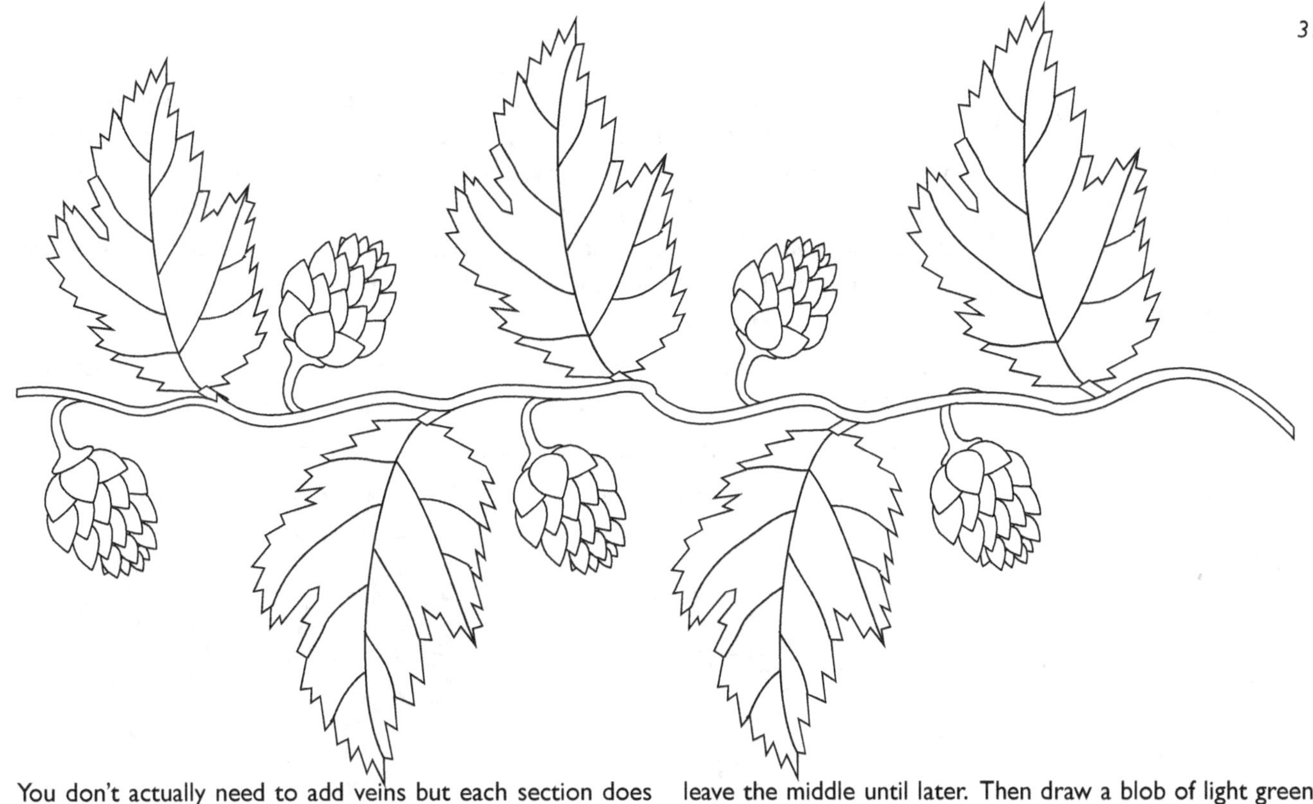

You don't actually need to add veins but each section does need to touch in order to adhere. To fill in the hops do a loop for each section each one overlapping the next and then, as they get bigger, infill with the extruded blob technique (see page 7).

To draw the flowers on the bramble/blackberry plants, loop and infill without blobbing on the flowers and leave the middle until later. Then draw a blob of light green in the middle. The berries are made simply by making small repetitive blobs. Touch the page and allow the plastic to flow for a moment only then release the feed and repeat. The spines are a bit difficult. Press the pen against the stem. Allow the plastic to flow for the shortest possible time (on a slow setting if you have one) then release and pull away quickly. This takes some practise. If you find it difficult, simply leave the spines off.

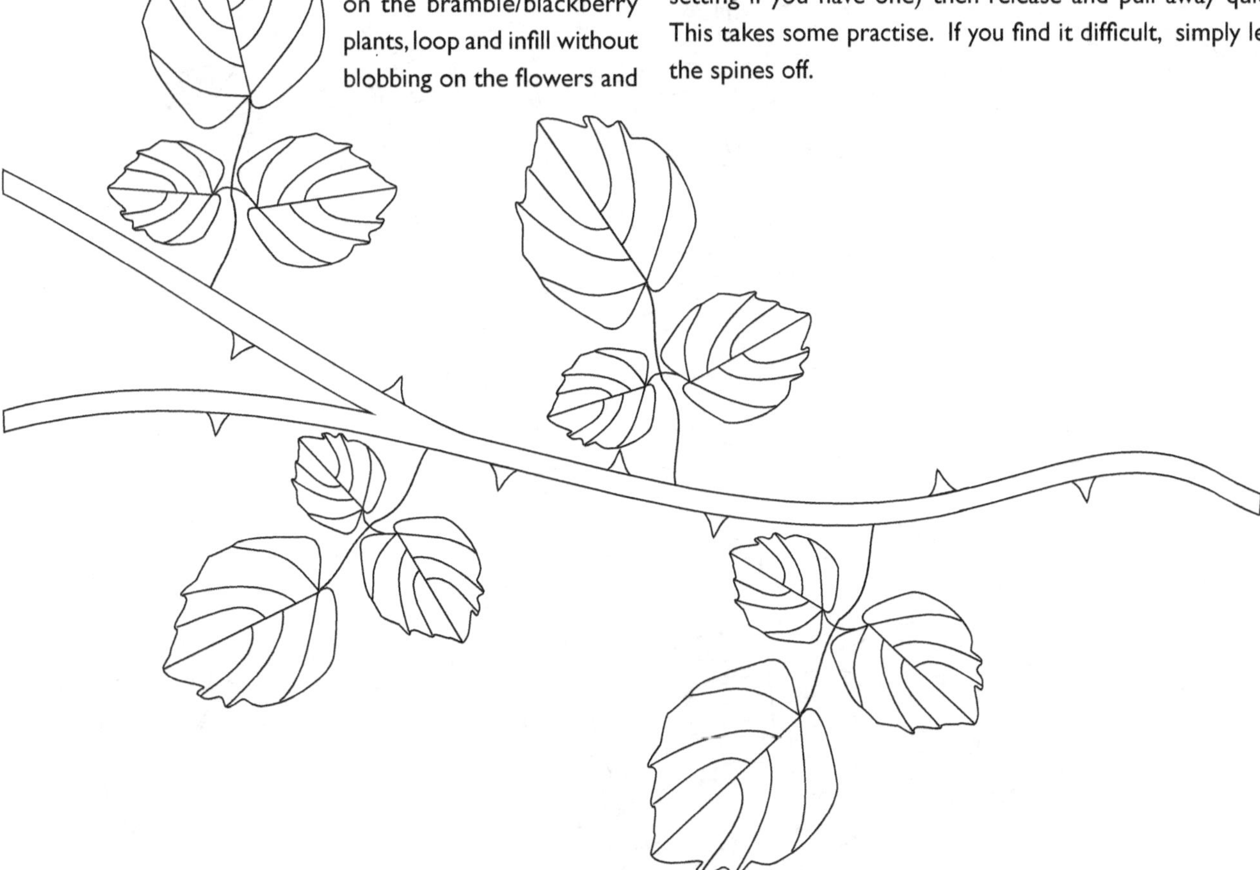

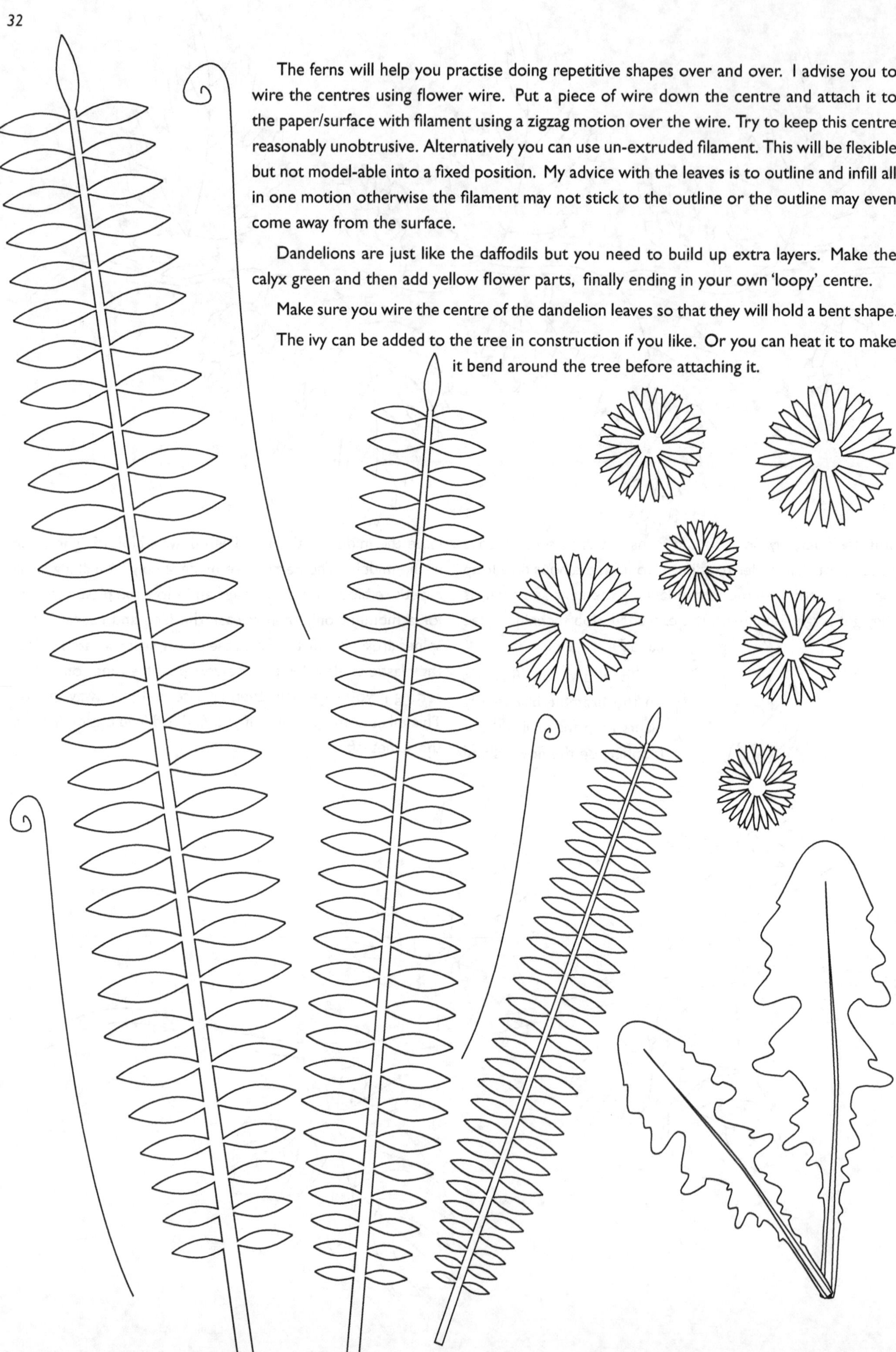

The ferns will help you practise doing repetitive shapes over and over. I advise you to wire the centres using flower wire. Put a piece of wire down the centre and attach it to the paper/surface with filament using a zigzag motion over the wire. Try to keep this centre reasonably unobtrusive. Alternatively you can use un-extruded filament. This will be flexible but not model-able into a fixed position. My advice with the leaves is to outline and infill all in one motion otherwise the filament may not stick to the outline or the outline may even come away from the surface.

Dandelions are just like the daffodils but you need to build up extra layers. Make the calyx green and then add yellow flower parts, finally ending in your own 'loopy' centre.

Make sure you wire the centre of the dandelion leaves so that they will hold a bent shape.

The ivy can be added to the tree in construction if you like. Or you can heat it to make it bend around the tree before attaching it.

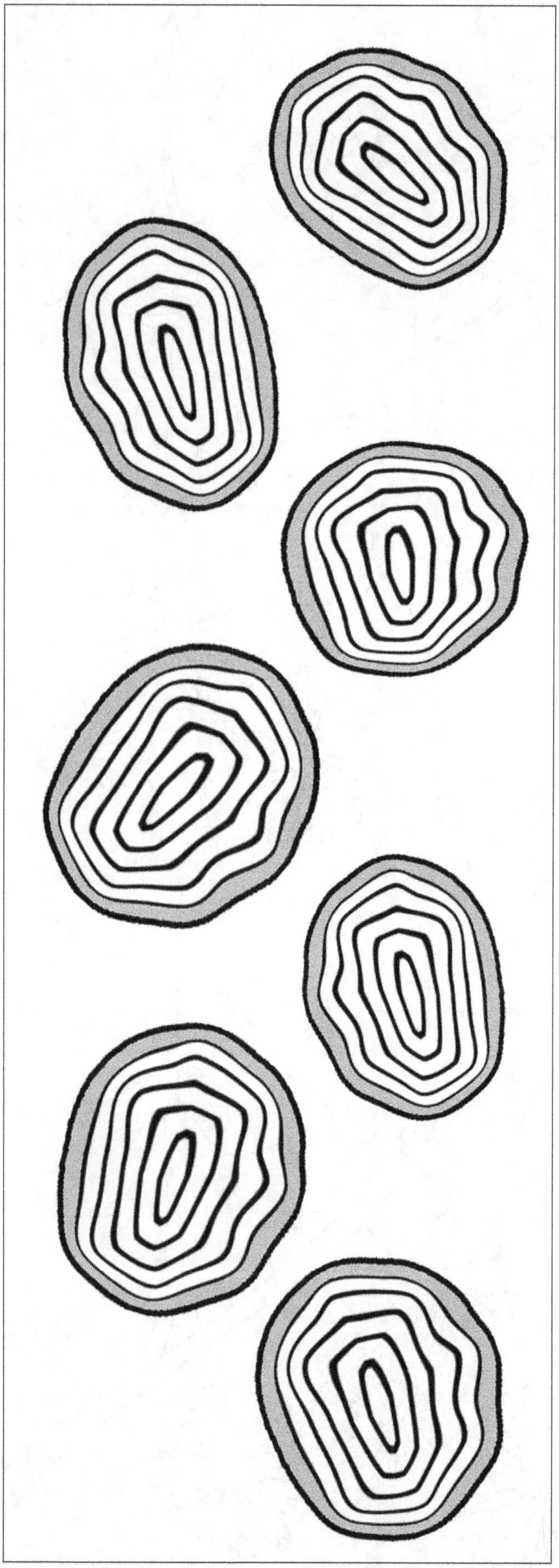

The wood end grain stepping stones are made using several different wood filaments from different suppliers. Lots of irritating changing of filaments here so I'd make extra! You could make wood block seats and even a table in the same way. You can buy sample lengths of various wood colours from a samples supplier and I think its worth doing for the results. I filled in between the stepping stones with very short loops of 2 greens to give it extra dimension.

For the coppicing I used barnyard brown by Ice Filaments. As you can see we've made 2 sides which match and a central support. You would be best tracing these through on to Tetra-pak card because the paper is really irritating to get off these twiggy bits. When made peel all the parts off and 'glue' them together over the support. Make the horseshoe in 2 parts as well. I used a dark grey for the main part of the shoe and black for the in fills. Remember the in fills are lower so 2 layers of the first colour and only one of the in fill colour. You will need to attach the horseshoe to the path. Use green filament and cover up the join with long grass.

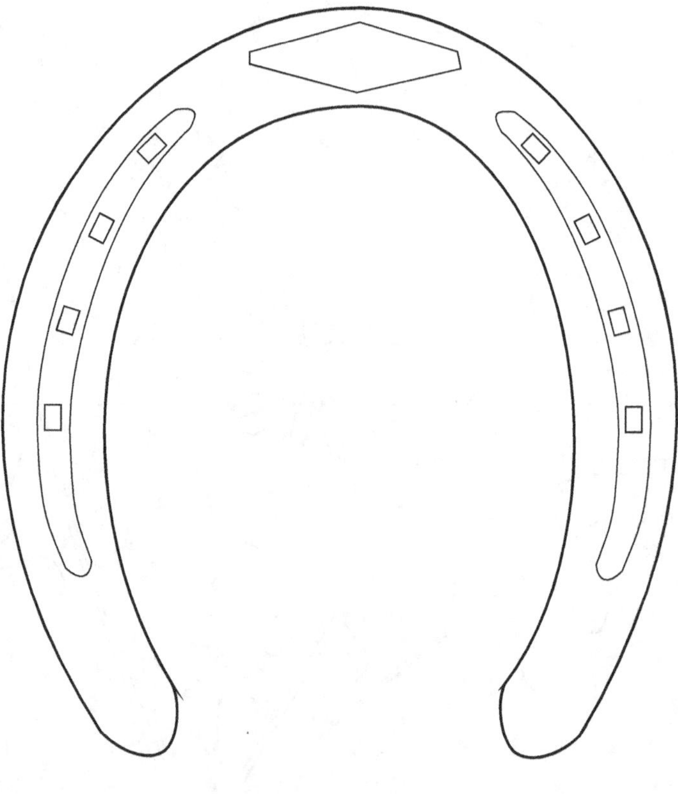

Coppice fencing & support

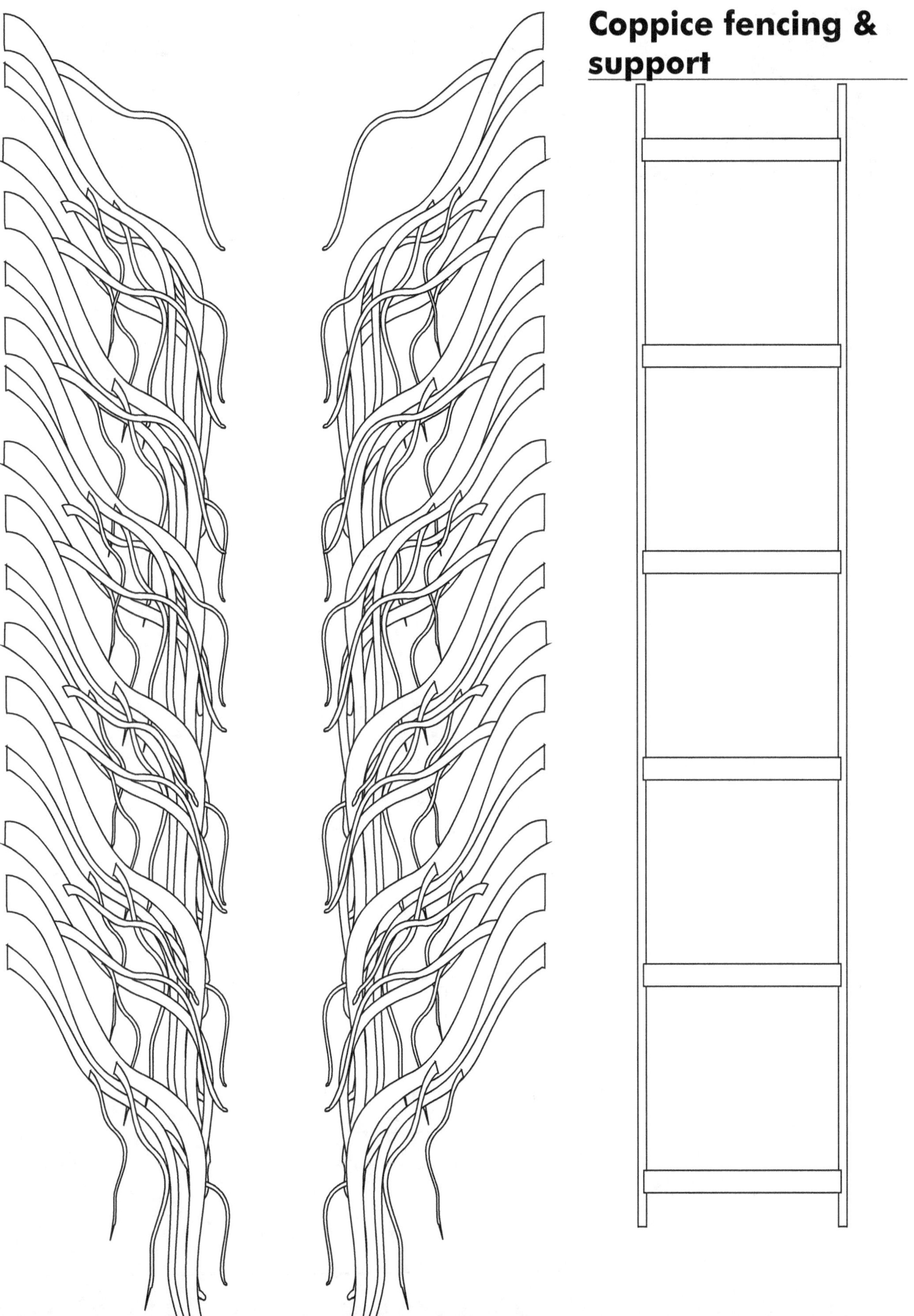

Old Boot House

The boot can be partly constructed on a 4" (10cm) diameter postal tube, although you can use 2 custard tins taped together. Tape one side to the tube and draw in the boot and its door and windows. Don't expect to get a smooth finish. It will never happen. You may also find that there are cracks and gaps, but it is an old boot! When you have completed one side (quite a long job) take it off and do the other side.

You can then peel the front part of the second side away and join the heel and back together while on the tube.

The toe section has to be drawn on Tetrapak card and taped into shape. I made the tongue part on Tetrapak card but I held it twisted a bit as I drew so that it wasn't too straight. When putting the boot together you may need to apply some heat to make it more flexible. A hot hairdryer or heat gun (very carefully applied!!!) may help. I did it without.

You're going to need some patience to fit the pieces together. I found I wanted a deeper boot so I then added a long inch wide (2cm) strip which turned out to be 2 entire lengths of a rectangular Tetrapak, and put a brown strip to simulate the rubber sole on the bottom. I used the sole piece to get the shape right but decided not to draw the sole itself. The laces are just un-treated filament.

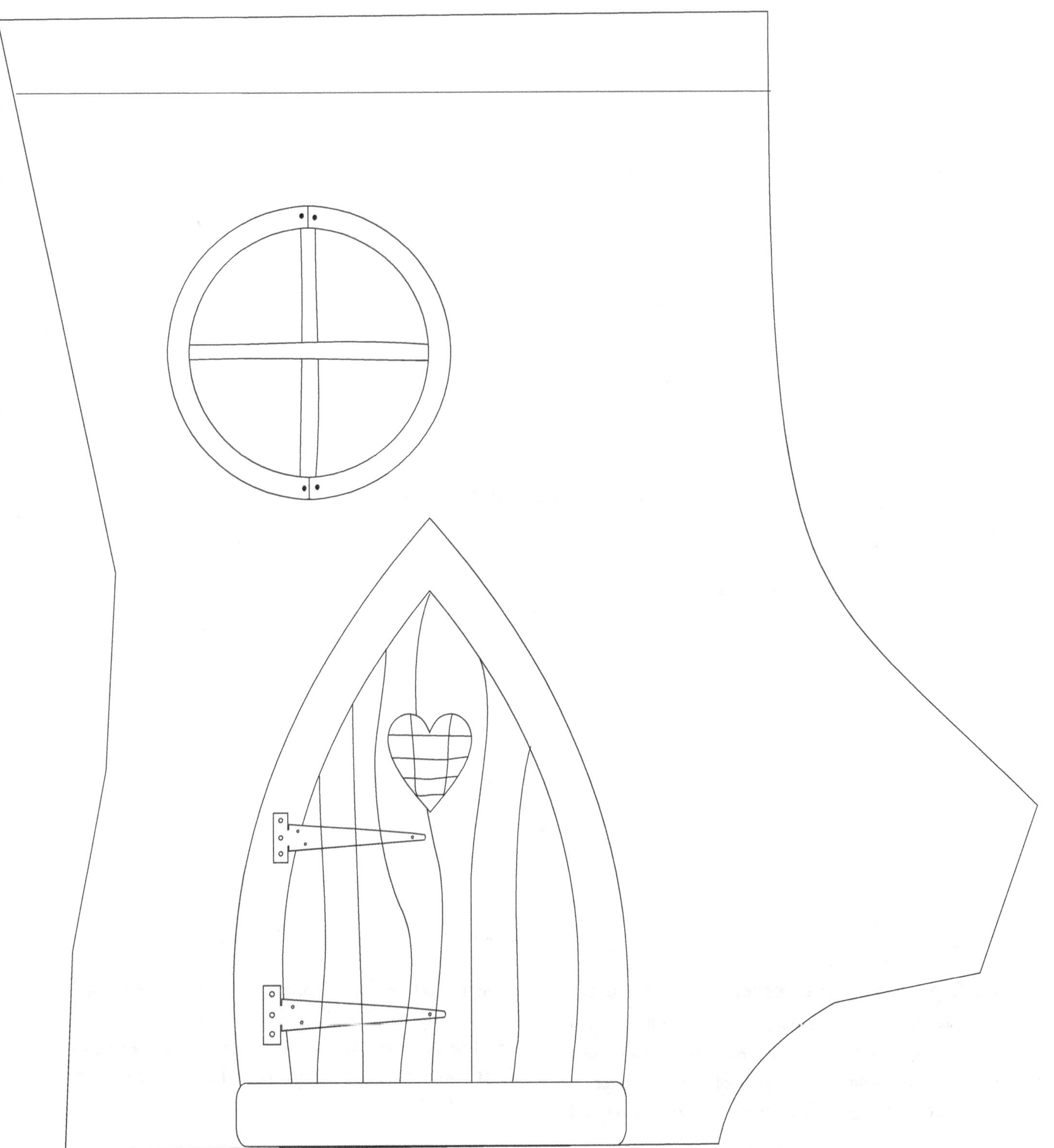

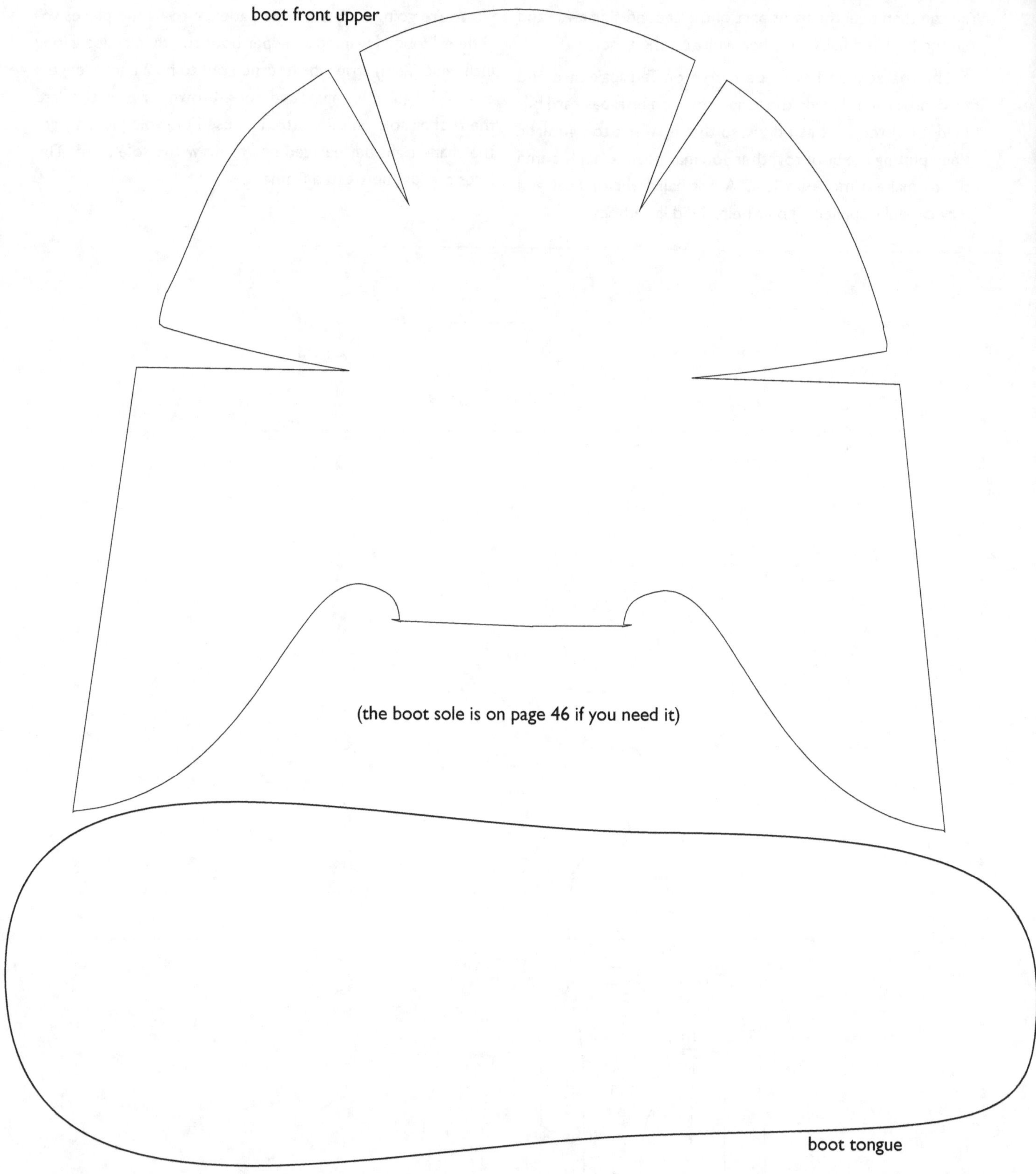

The Cigar box is an exercise in patience.

I used TreeD's 'Sandy'. With the pen set on fast flow (if you have that option) fill each section smoothly and patiently in a continuous motion making sure each line of filament pushes up against the last. The edges will come out slightly thicker and stronger. You will get a very good result with a good filament and lots of patience. Fold the box up with the paper backing still attached. Assemble the sections with extra filament leaving the lid at a wide enough angle to cover the top of the boot.

Join here

Join here

Join here

Join here

Use this cigar box for the roof of the boot house

CIGARS

Poppies, Wheat & Michelmas Daisies

The flower petals. You can choose whether to colour the middle in black or leave it all the same colour. Poppies made in 3D pen will never be as fine as we'd really like them, but you can make them as thin and delicate as possible by making the pen tip score through the filament as it extrudes. Work from the centre of the petals outwards in a fan shape making sure each filament sticks to the next, at least in the middle and at the edge. When you have made each set of petals remove them from the surface. Find a curved heat proof surface to put them on or even the handle of a wooden spoon and warm them with a hair dryer or heat gun until they soften and change into a curved form.

Add the petals to the 'cup' on the stem by filling the hole using green or black filament. Each poppy has 2 sets of petals one at 90 degrees to the other. Then add the poppy centre. Finally dot some green around the outside of the centre.

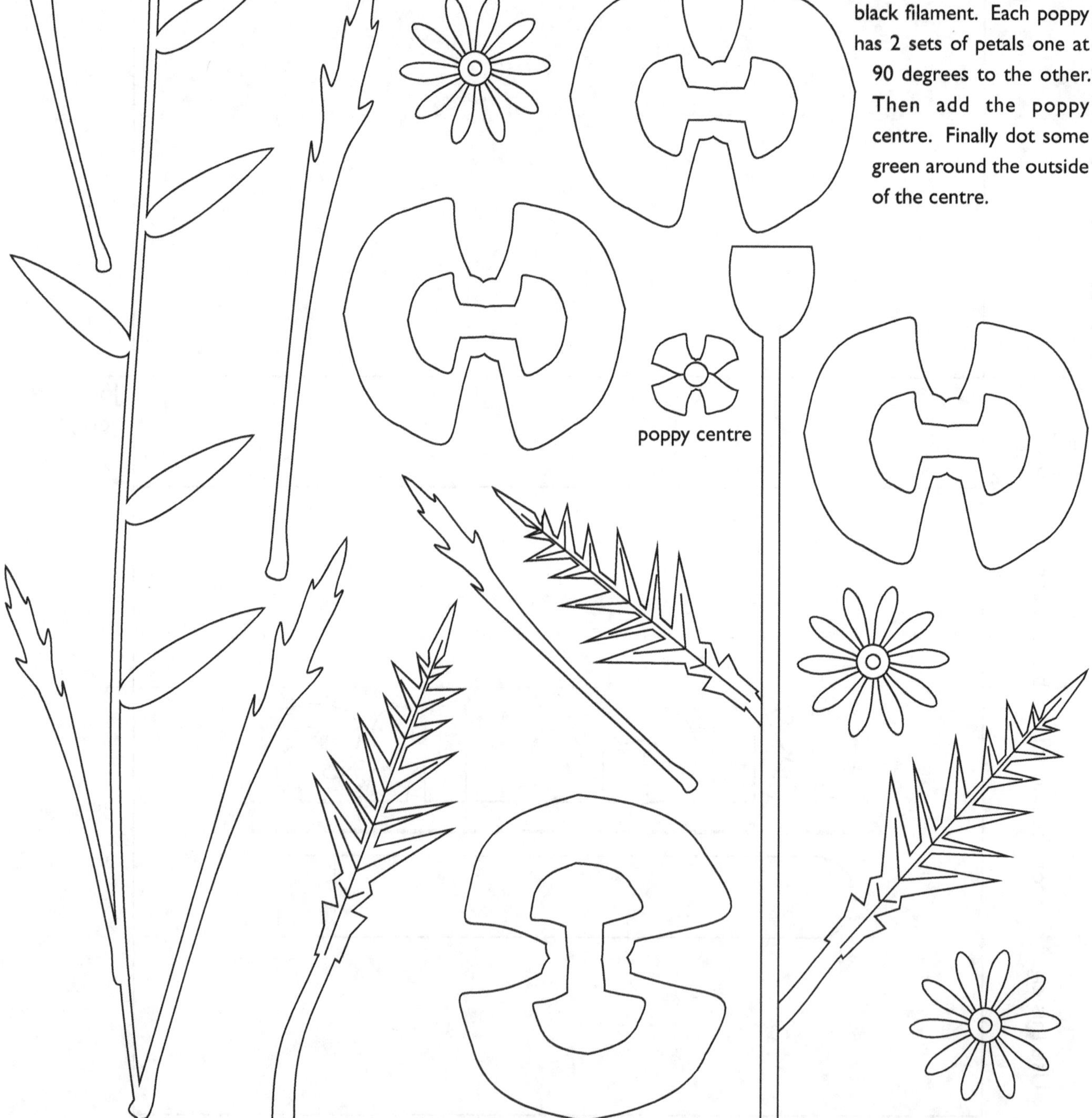

Weeds

A little more advanced. This page has some complicated and delicate little weeds but they should be easier to handle when you are used to using the pen. The stem on the far left is for the chick weed. That's the stuff we call 'sticky weed'. The 4 biggest star shapes should be made in green and threaded on to the stem. The little loopy bits are a simplified version of the bundles of flowers but are also in green. You can also add side stems with loop ends and the smaller stars threaded on.

The small 5 petal flowers can be made half green and half pink and one added over the other to add to very fine stems in the leaf nodes on the plant on the far right.

The delicate plant second left can be elongated as long as you want as it has a very creeping habit. I really enjoyed making this one and made good use of the staining left on the inside of the pen when changing from one colour to the next. See top tips on page 47

Insects

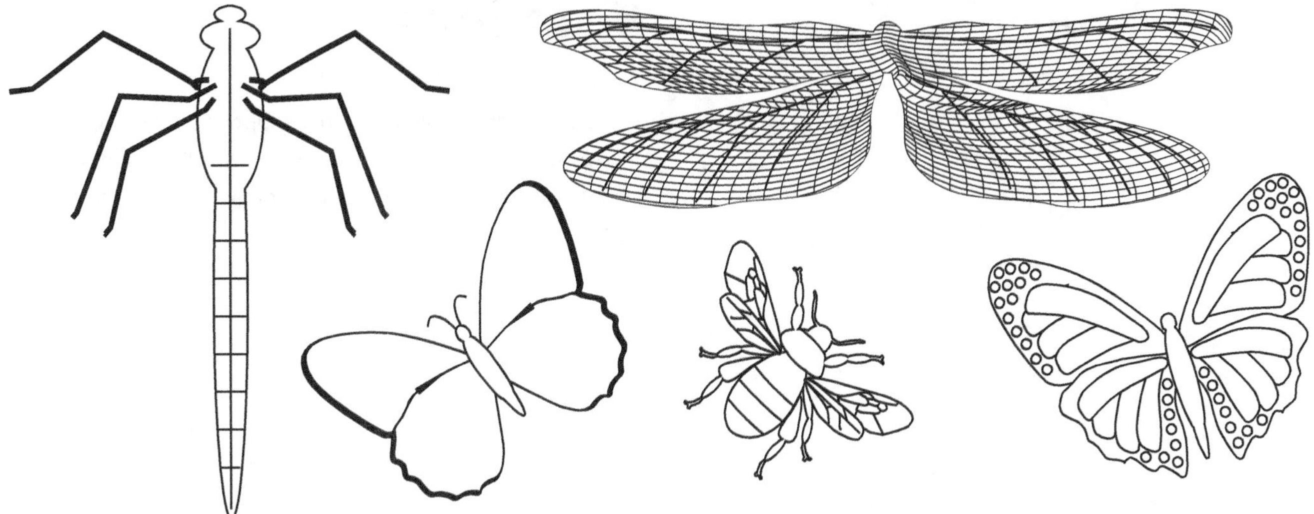

The toner take-up technique

This works best on delicate elements particularly where you need a very translucent or light colour but the detail in 3D pen can be a little clumsy. I use it on dragonflies, butterflies and plants to leave outlines and details.

Draw the outline of the object directly on to the photocopied paper and fill in with your colour choice. You will need to peel and then soak off the paper from the back of your pen drawing. The toner on the paper is taken up by the molten plastic leaving delightful outlines and details.

Toner take-up in colour

I was wondering how to do this in other colours if I wanted while still putting the design books out in black and white so people can choose their colours. Frank came up with the simple but clever idea of simply colouring in a first generation photocopy with good strong felt pens, then photocopying again and simply working over your colour photocopy. This works particularly well with butterfly and dragonfly wings and subtle flower colour shading. Polymer clay artists probably already use this technique (and if not, why not?!) but I never have until now and I think its an interesting technique for 3D pen work.

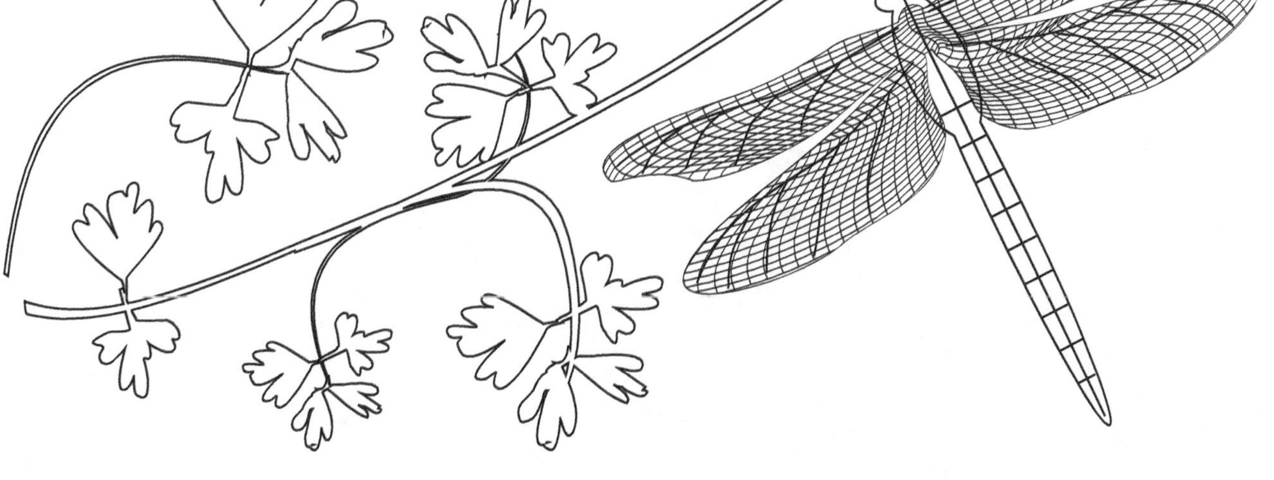

Boot Sole

You may need this for extra support when shaping the main boot. You can also cut an extra strip all around the sole for additional height measuring approx 2cm high by taping together several pieces of paper.

Top Tips

Thinking about colour and translucency.

You can use the tendency of some of the darker colours to leave a stain in the body of the pen to your advantage. When using semi translucent whites and naturals you can 'tint' them to produce some really delicate flower colours. These tinted colours don't last long so you will have to plan which jobs you do in which sequence in order to take advantage of this. For example after doing the gerbera centre in magenta I moved on to do the very delicate pink weed flowers on page 42. I also used this effect on some of the bluebells because it was difficult to find an appropriate bluebell colour.

If you can find colours which are really closely related you can add extra interest to your flowers. For example I made some of the dandelion flowers with a slightly brighter more acidic and translucent yellow in the centre. The outer edges then looked 'older'.

I couldn't find a really translucent red when making my redcurrants but for a really good effect they do need to be done with a translucent red.

Painting afterwards

One thing which I don't do, which you might choose to, is painting your work after constructing it. For example if you really can't buy the colour of filament that you want. Spray and oil colours will usually stick well to filaments. Water based paints may not. You will not be able to achieve any translucency when painting.

Displaying your fairy houses

Absolutely the best base for displaying your work and even working out your 'plan' is Oasis dried flower foam. I stuck mine on a hardboard base board and sprinkled with scenic materials which are available from railway modelling suppliers. If the scene is for adults or older children you can use pins around the edge to hold the grass on or you can glue long grass up the edges.

Children (not for very young children) will absolutely love planting and re-planting the flowers and moving the houses so if the scene is for children its worth considering the base as wholly disposable and your work as repeatable as delicate parts will get broken.

Fairies!

I'm not a fan of dolls in scenes but if you want to people the scene Barbie do a miniature and a 3" Barbie. This "worlds smallest" size is approximately 1/24th scale and therefore correct for these houses. And you can make her wings using translucent filament over either the dragonfly or butterfly wings template. Plain photocopy or coloured in and photocopied. Or my polymer clay using friends might like to use liquid polymer over coloured in examples. However the slightly bigger Barbie, which sometimes actually comes in a fairy costume, would be great for children who don't care quite so much about scale. And after all this book is hardly scale-ist! I bought a mini Barbie from Lidl and a micro one from a shop in Malaga station, but it's worth looking online.

Index

Biographies

Angie Scarr is better known as a polymer clay miniaturist specialising in miniature ingredients. Her first two books Making Miniature Food and Market Stalls Miniature Food Masterclass have been best sellers for GMC books and together with husband Frank Fisher she has recently self published Angie Scarr's Colour Book and The Miniature Gardens Book and two smaller books which revisit her early 'challenge' magazine articles.

Frank, is a self-confessed 'computer geek' with a history of recording music, writing database driven websites and recently running the Angie Scarr Miniatures business. He and Angie have worked together on the self published books and Frank has encouraged other craftspeople to self publish too.

Angie and Frank live in a partly self-built home in rural Andalucia, Spain and divide their time between trying to finish the build, making and teaching miniature crafts, writing books and producing YouTube videos and recently designing a range of stencils for polymer clay flowers. This latest book is a departure from the more perfectionist miniatures into a more 'just for fun' approach, and is their first co-authored book.

Thanks & Ackowledgements

Thanks for the inspiration to write this book my daughter (Frank's stepdaughter) Kira Swales who bought me my first 3D pen.

Angie Grace designer of adult colouring books.

Rigid Ink who encouraged me and helped me find some of the best filaments and put me in touch with Barbara. Another hispanophile and 3D pen user.

Barbara Taylor Harris herself who shared her ideas with me as I shared my polymer ideas with her one weekend in 2016. Barbara has constantly shared knowledge of tools and materials and we've exchanged loads of materials. Barbara has sent me pens to help me understand the differences between pens. Barbara has recently written a study book on 3D pen art.

Joanna Beresford's Secret Garden colouring book which inspired me when I was thinking of the colouring book to 3D pen idea.

Frank and I would both like to thank Eileen (Frank's mum) and other family members and friends for lots of support over the two years while I was struggling with ill health. The ill health is forgotten but the support never is.

Information, further reading and watching

My YouTube channel
Videos from archive material made back in the days when the internet was newborn and YouTube wasn't even thought of, to up to date projects & some further explanations on projects in this book.
www.youtube.com/user/angiescarr

My Facebook page
www.facebook.com/angiescarr.miniatures

My Pinterest page
www.pinterest.co.uk/angiescarr/

My Instagram page
www.instagram.com/angiescarr

And finally my website where you can find all these and more
www.angiescarr.co.uk

Other 3D pen books

Barbara Taylor Harris has written 2 books which are sold together
barbara@theoldparsonage.net

Go Beyond Doodling, Make 3D Pen Art The Ultimate 3D Pen Creation Guide Instruction book
ISBN 978-1-9996477-0-4
& Go Beyond Doodling, Make 3D Pen Art The Ultimate 3D Pen Companion Template Guide
ISBN 978-1-9996477-1-1

Barbara's books take you step by step in a textbook format towards creating pieces of 3D Art and is suitable for both individuals and teachers.

Suppliers

3D pen & accessories

3d pens are readily available on eBay and Amazon. So far we haven't found that the expensive ones compare favourably with the cheaper ones. However choice of filaments is important. You should always use ABS with the cheaper machines except where specified (e.g. wood and stone filaments may not be available as ABS). The pen used in this book is Idrawing ID-161 www.amazon.com/gp/product/B077GW342Y

Filaments (as used in this book)

Natural green filaments:

Olive & Khaki rigidink   https://rigid.ink/

Light green (Gracious Green) Ice filaments http://www.icefilaments.com/

Mid green (green) - Verbatim

Dark mid green (Vert) Dailyfil (French company)

Wood filaments:

Barnyard brown and Grasshopper green - Ice filaments

Stone:

'Sandy' etc Treed http://treedfilaments.com/3d-printing-filaments

Sample suppliers:- https://globalfsd.com https://shop.3dfilaprint.com

Coloured filaments:

From a variety of the suppliers above and from 'bundles' on Amazon.

For links to suppliers please check out our website suppliers page at www.angiescarr.co.uk/suppliers

Flower wires

Vanilla Valley (online supplier of cake decorating materials)